Congressional
Research
Service

U.S. Trade and Investment in the Middle East and North Africa: Overview and Issues for Congress

Rebecca M. Nelson, Coordinator
Analyst in International Trade and Finance

Mary Jane Bolle
Specialist in International Trade and Finance

Shayerah Ilias Akhtar
Specialist in International Trade and Finance

February 28, 2013

Congressional Research Service

7-5700

www.crs.gov

R42153

CRS Report for Congress ———————————————————

Prepared for Members and Committees of Congress

Summary

U.S. interest in deepening economic ties with certain countries in the Middle East and North Africa (MENA) has increased in light of the political unrest and transitions that have swept the region since early 2011. Policymakers in Congress and the Obama Administration are discussing ways that U.S. trade and investment can bolster long-term economic growth in the region. In May 2011, President Obama announced the MENA "Trade and Investment Partnership Initiative" (MENA-TIP), through which various federal government agencies are engaged in efforts to enhance trade and investment with the region. Such activities are in line with longstanding U.S. trade policy goals and measures. Some Members of Congress have called for deeper economic ties with MENA countries undergoing political change. However, continued political uncertainty and changing security environments in the region have prompted greater scrutiny of U.S. engagement. This report analyzes policy approaches that the Congress might consider concerning U.S.-MENA trade and investment.

MENA Economies and Integration in the Global Economy

Economic performance in the MENA as a whole lags behind other regions in the world in terms of gross domestic product (GDP) per capita (living standards), employment, and economic diversification, despite the fact that several MENA countries are major producers of oil and natural gas. Limited integration in the global economy is frequently cited as an obstacle to the region's overall economic development. MENA's trade with the world is concentrated in a small number of products (oil exports and imports of manufactured goods) and among a small number of trading partners (particularly the European Union). Tariffs also remain high in some MENA countries and intra-regional trade and investment flows are relatively low. With regard to the United States, the MENA region accounts for less than 5% of U.S. total trade and 1% of U.S. foreign direct investment (FDI) outflows. U.S. businesses face a number of non-tariff barriers, such as lack of transparency, bureaucratic red tape, corruption, weak rule of law, and differences in business cultures.

Policy Approaches and Challenges

Current U.S. trade and investment policies with MENA countries are quite varied. The United States has free trade agreements (FTAs) with five MENA countries (Bahrain, Israel, Jordan, Morocco, and Oman), but more limited ties with other countries, such as Libya, which is not a member of the World Trade Organization (WTO). Important exceptions to overall U.S. trade policy objectives in the region are Iran and Syria, which are both subject to trade sanctions.

Analysts disagree about the merits of deepening U.S. trade and investment ties with the MENA region. Some analysts maintain that new trade and investment agreements help anchor domestic reforms, such as in governance and rule of law; support sound economic growth; are a cost-effective way to support transitioning countries in an environment of budgetary constraints; and could promote U.S. exports and investment. Others argue that the empirical record between economic openness and democracy is weak and that it is unclear whether protesters in various Arab countries favor more economic liberalization, which they sometimes associate with corruption, inflation, and inequality. They also argue that political uncertainty in the region, such as the fluidity of Egypt's political transition, merits a "wait-and-see" approach before proceeding with substantial policy changes.

The 113th Congress could consider a number of approaches regarding U.S. trade and investment with the region, including:

- maintaining the status quo until the impact of the political changes in MENA countries is clear;

- providing technical assistance to countries working towards WTO membership, as well as trade capacity building support to countries working to implement WTO commitments;

- negotiating new trade and/or investment agreements with countries in the region that do not already have them, such as Egypt and Tunisia;

- utilizing existing trade frameworks for greater dialogue and progress on trade and investment and encouraging regional integration;

- reauthorizing existing trade preferences through the Generalized System of Preferences (GSP) program or creating a U.S. trade preference program, differing from GSP, that grants preferential market access to exports from MENA countries; and

- increasing assistance from federal export and investment promotion agencies to the region.

In considering such approaches, some questions that could arise include:

- Should the U.S. government promote expanded trade and investment in the near-term in order to support democratic transitions, or should it wait until the political situation stabilizes in various countries? To what extent should the United States balance a regional approach of increased trade and investment with more tailored policies to the specific needs of individual countries?

- To what extent should the United States cooperate with the European Union or others on trade and investment in the MENA region?

Are existing U.S. frameworks and agreements on trade and investment with MENA countries benefitting the region, and achieving the intended objectives? What lessons can be learned from past U.S. efforts to promote trade and investment? How effective are current efforts to expand trade and investment under the MENA-TIP initiative?

Contents

Figures

Tables

Appendixes

Contacts

Introduction

The political unrest and transitions that have swept through several countries in the Middle East and North Africa (MENA) since early 2011—often referred to as the "Arab Spring" or "Arab Awakening"—have prompted the United States, along with the broader international community, to discuss approaches and take actions to support democratic political transitions in the region.[1] A key focus is the role that economic growth can play in solidifying and supporting political transitions in the region.

Calls for greater U.S. trade and investment with the region in support of economic growth have come from policymakers in the Administration and Congress. In May 2011, President Obama announced the MENA "Trade and Investment Partnership Initiative" (MENA-TIP) to facilitate trade and investment with the region. The initiative has a primary focus on Egypt, Jordan, Morocco, and Tunisia.[2] Within Congress, some Members have called for new free trade agreements (FTAs) with Egypt and Tunisia, and deeper economic ties with Libya.[3]

Presently, U.S. trade and investment policy in the region is focused on using trade and investment to foster economic growth, promote greater economic reforms, provide support for successful and stable democratic transitions, and generally support U.S. foreign policy objectives.[4] The U.S. government is pursuing such efforts both as part of the MENA-TIP initiative and through broader or longstanding U.S. trade policy measures. Measures to bolster trade and investment ties are often long-term in nature, and could build on other shorter-term measures to support transitioning countries.[5] However, continued political uncertainty and changing security environments in the region could prompt greater scrutiny of U.S. engagement, as policymakers grapple with questions of timing, feasibility, and political support for such efforts.[6]

Congress has oversight, authorization, and appropriation responsibilities related to U.S. trade and investment policy. New U.S. trade and investment initiatives with the MENA region could require congressional involvement. For example, legislative action would be needed to implement new

---

[1] There is no standard definition of which countries belong to the Middle East and North Africa (MENA) region; different organizations define the region differently. This report primarily relies on the categorization used by the World Bank. The World Bank defines the MENA region to include Algeria, Bahrain, Djibouti, Egypt, Iran, Iraq, Israel, Jordan, Kuwait, Lebanon, Libya, Malta, Morocco, Oman, Qatar, Saudi Arabia, Syria, Tunisia, the United Arab Emirates (UAE), the West Bank, and Yemen. Some may disagree with the categorization; for example, Malta, may be a particular point of contention because it is a member of the European Union (EU). However, given the data constraints for the MENA region and the availability of data from the World Bank, the World Bank's categorization is used in this report.

[2] Office of the Press Secretary, "Remarks by the President on the Middle East and North Africa," The White House, State Department, Washington, DC, May 19, 2011, http://www.whitehouse.gov/the-press-office/2011/05/19/remarks-president-middle-east-and-north-africa.

[3] For example, see Prepared Remarks of Senator Joseph Lieberman, Carnegie Endowment for International Peace, July 22, 2011, http://carnegieendowment.org/files/Lieberman_Prepared_Remarks.pdf; John McCain, Lindsey Graham, Mark Kirk, and Marco Rubio, "The Promise of a Pro-American Libya," *Wall Street Journal,* October 7, 2011. In addition, in November 2011, Representative Dreier introduced a resolution, co-sponsored by Representative Meeks, that calls for the United States to initiate free trade agreement (FTA) negotiations with Egypt (H.Res. 472).

[4] In this report, terms such as "trade policy" or "trade relations" refer to policies related to both trade and investment.

[5] For examples of other approaches in the context of Egypt, see CRS Report RL33003, *Egypt: Background and U.S. Relations*, by Jeremy M. Sharp.

[6] CRS Report R42393, *Change in the Middle East: Implications for U.S. Policy*, coordinated by Christopher M. Blanchard.

---

free trade agreements. Congress also may want to exercise oversight over any changes to government programs that promote U.S. trade and investment.

The structure of this report is as follows:

- The report begins with background and analysis for policymakers considering a re-evaluation of U.S. trade and investment in the MENA in light of political change in the region. In particular, the report examines the economic challenges facing many countries in the region and the area's limited economic integration—both in the world economy, including relatively weak economic ties with the United States, and in the MENA regional economy.

- The report then analyzes current U.S. trade and investment policy efforts in the region and various policy options for increasing trade and investment with MENA countries.

- The report concludes by discussing: 1) the premise of the policy agenda, specifically whether increased trade and investment can support or lead to successful democratic transitions and political stability; and 2) if such a policy agenda is pursued, possible implementation questions that policymakers may face.

Figure 1. Map of Middle East and North Africa (MENA)

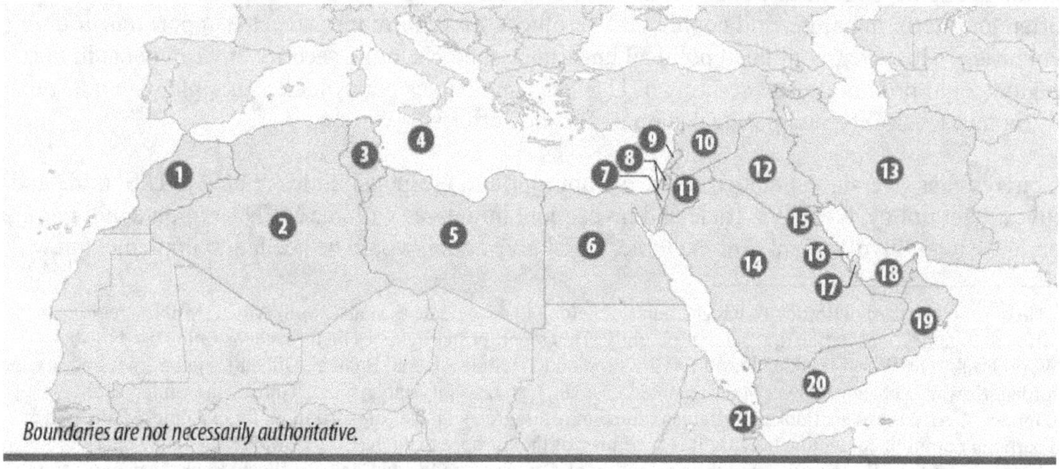

Boundaries are not necessarily authoritative.

MENA Countries	Algeria 2 Bahrain 16 Dijibouti 21 Egypt 6 Iran 13	Iraq 12 Israel 7 Jordan 11 Kuwait 15 Lebanon 9	Libya 5 Malta 4 Morocco 1 Oman 19 Qatar 17	Saudi Arabia 14 Syria 10 Tunisia 3 United Arab Emirates 18	West Bank/ Gaza Strip 8 Yemen 20

Source: CRS.

Note: World Bank definition of the MENA. For more information, see footnote 1.

Economic Challenges in the MENA Region

Weak Economic Development Despite Abundant Natural Resources

As a whole, the MENA region lags behind other regions on many key economic indicators (**Figure 2**). In 2011, the region accounted for 5.6% of the world's total population, but its economic output is disproportionately smaller, accounting for just 4.4% of the world's gross domestic product (GDP). Additionally, the region's GDP per capita in 2011 ($7,831) was lower than those of Latin America and the Caribbean ($9,754) and East Asia and the Pacific ($8,475). The region generally has poorly developed manufacturing and service sectors; the value-added of manufacturing and services relative to GDP in MENA in 2010 was the smallest in the world. Weak economic opportunities, combined with one of the fastest growing populations in the world, have resulted in high levels of unemployment. Unemployment in the region was 9.7% in 2008, more than double the unemployment rate in East Asia and the Pacific (4.7%) in 2009. Unemployment among youth in particular is a challenge. For example, in 2009, youth (15-24 year olds) unemployment was 27% in Jordan, and 22% in Morocco. By contrast, youth unemployment in Thailand, which has a similar GDP per capita to Jordan's, was markedly lower at 4.3% in 2009.[7]

While several countries in the region are rich in natural resources, especially oil and natural gas, the revenues from these resources have been poorly utilized and the development of other production and export industries has lagged. MENA countries produced 30% of the world's oil and 22% of the world's natural gas in 2011.[8] Oil production is concentrated in Algeria, Bahrain, Iran, Iraq, Kuwait, Libya, Oman, Qatar, Saudi Arabia, the United Arab Emirates (UAE), and Yemen. Other countries in the region typically import more oil than they produce, or do not produce any oil at all. The mismatch between endowments of natural resources and weak economic development is frequently called a "resource curse," since endowments of natural resources like oil seem to have deterred, rather than jumpstarted, broad economic development in many countries and potentially exacerbated inequality. In some countries, notably in the oil-rich Gulf region, governments are now actively seeking to leverage state oil export revenues to support the development of non-hydrocarbon economic sectors and the expansion of employment opportunities. In countries where energy resources must be imported, governments may struggle with fiscal pressures.

---

[7] World Bank, *World Development Indicators*.

[8] U.S. Energy Information Administration, *International Energy Statistics*. Calculations based on total oil supply and gross natural gas production, using World Bank regional grouping.

Figure 2. The MENA Economy in Comparative Perspective: Key Indicators

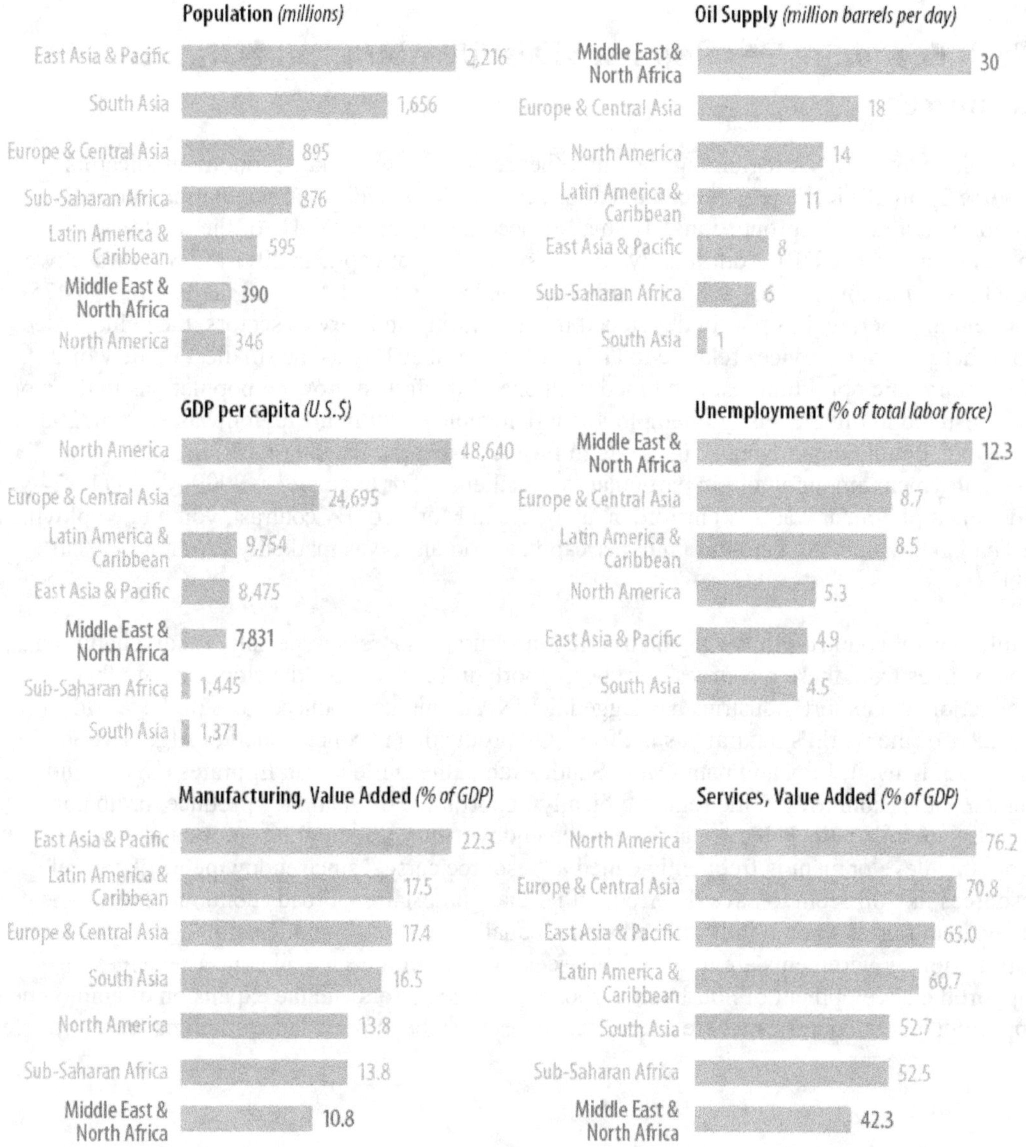

Population *(millions)*

East Asia & Pacific	2,216
South Asia	1,656
Europe & Central Asia	895
Sub-Saharan Africa	876
Latin America & Caribbean	595
Middle East & North Africa	390
North America	346

Oil Supply *(million barrels per day)*

Middle East & North Africa	30
Europe & Central Asia	18
North America	14
Latin America & Caribbean	11
East Asia & Pacific	8
Sub-Saharan Africa	6
South Asia	1

GDP per capita *(U.S.$)*

North America	48,640
Europe & Central Asia	24,695
Latin America & Caribbean	9,754
East Asia & Pacific	8,475
Middle East & North Africa	7,831
Sub-Saharan Africa	1,445
South Asia	1,371

Unemployment *(% of total labor force)*

Middle East & North Africa	12.3
Europe & Central Asia	8.7
Latin America & Caribbean	8.5
North America	5.3
East Asia & Pacific	4.9
South Asia	4.5

Manufacturing, Value Added *(% of GDP)*

East Asia & Pacific	22.3
Latin America & Caribbean	17.5
Europe & Central Asia	17.4
South Asia	16.5
North America	13.8
Sub-Saharan Africa	13.8
Middle East & North Africa	10.8

Services, Value Added *(% of GDP)*

North America	76.2
Europe & Central Asia	70.8
East Asia & Pacific	65.0
Latin America & Caribbean	60.7
South Asia	52.7
Sub-Saharan Africa	52.5
Middle East & North Africa	42.3

Source: World Bank, *World Development Indicators*; U.S. Energy Information Administration, *International Energy Statistics*.

Notes: Data are for the most recent year available. Population, oil production, and GDP per capita data are for 2011; unemployment data are for 2005; and service and manufacturing data are for 2010. Unemployment data for the Sub-Saharan Africa region as a whole are not available.

Obstacles to Development

Numerous explanations have been put forward to explain why economic development in the MENA region has lagged behind other regions.[9] For example, it has been argued that:

- **Weak integration in the global economy** has prevented the region from reaping the opportunities of globalization;

- **"Easy money" from natural resources** in some MENA countries has provided few incentives to develop sound economic policies or other productive industries, with the benefits of natural resources going to a few and not the public at large;

- **Non-democratic political institutions** have stifled innovation and economic competition, leading to slow growth and distortions in the economy;

- **A weak business environment**, stemming from heavy government involvement in the economy, red tape, corruption, and weak rule of law, has deterred foreign investment;

- **A weak educational system** has not equipped youth in the region with the skills demanded by the private sector in a competitive global environment;

- **Subsidies and lack of government infrastructure spending**, with large portions of the budget going to defense and subsidies for basic needs, creates distortions in the economy; and

- **Women constitute a low proportion of the labor force,** preventing the region from tapping all its productive potential.

Important Caveats: Areas of Success, and Heterogeneity Among Countries

Despite the economic challenges faced by the region as a whole, it is important to note that there have been some areas of economic success. Appreciating economic diversity among the MENA economies may have implications for the types of economic policies that might be pursued to bolster growth in the region, and suggests that policy solutions may need to be tailored to the specific circumstances of each economy.

For example, the World Bank and the International Monetary Fund (IMF) have applauded success on various social indicators of well-being and macroeconomic stability for the region.[10] In 2010,

---

[9] For example, see Marcus Noland and Howard Pack, "The Arab Economies in a Changing World," *Peterson Institute for International Economics*, June 2007, http://bookstore.piie.com/book-store/3931.html; United Nations, "Arab Human Development Report 2002: Creating Opportunities for Future Generations," 2002, http://www.arab-hdr.org/publications/other/ahdr/ahdr2002e.pdf; Howard Schneider, "Arab Nations Lag Behind Rest of World Economically, Despite Oil and Natural Gas," *Washington Post*, February 23, 2011; and Arvind Subramanian, "Arab Spring Will Not See an Economic Boom," *Financial Times*, February 21, 2011, http://www.iie.com/publications/opeds/oped.cfm?ResearchID=1770.

[10] For example, see International Monetary Fund (IMF), "IMF Note on Economic Transformation in MENA: Delivering on the Promise of Shared Prosperity," May 27, 2011, Prepared for the G-8 Summit in Deauville, France, http://www.imf.org/external/np/g8/052611.htm; and World Bank, "Middle East and North Africa Regional Brief," September 2011, http://go.worldbank.org/1JVC0DGRS0.

---

the MENA had a life expectancy of 72 years and a primary education completion rate of 91%, and an under-5 mortality rate of 31 per 1,000 births. Absolute poverty in the region is also relatively low, with approximately 4% of the population living on $1.25 a day.[11] Additionally, the IMF has noted that, over the past two decades, the region has generally been successful in reining in inflation, improving trade balances, and reducing public debt levels. However, some countries undergoing political transition are experiencing macroeconomic instability.

Substantial diversity also exists in the region, and some countries have achieved greater levels of economic success than others (**Table 1**). For example, some of the region's small, oil-exporting countries are among the richest countries in the world; GDP per capita is higher in Kuwait and Qatar ($62,664 and $92,501 respectively in 2011) than in the United States ($48,111 in 2011). Likewise, some countries have stronger political and legal institutions than others; according to the World Bank's *Worldwide Governance Indicators*, Qatar ranked in the 74th percentile among countries worldwide in strength of rule of law in 2011.[12] Economic reforms have taken root in some countries; in the World Bank's *Doing Business* Report, Saudi Arabia is ranked as the 22nd easiest country in the world in which to do business.[13] While female participation in the labor force is low in many countries, women made up 47% of the labor force in Israel in 2010.

Finally, some countries in the region continue to grapple with various social challenges and macroeconomic stability, areas where the region as a whole is viewed as having succeeded. For example, poverty in Egypt is relatively high, with nearly one in six Egyptians (15.4%) living on less than $2 a day in 2008. The under-5 mortality rate in Yemen was 77 per 1,000 births in 2011, more than twice than the average for the region as a whole. In terms of macroeconomic stability, Lebanon has a high level of public debt (forecasted to be 135% of GDP in 2013), and Egypt is running a large budget deficit (forecasted to be 9.8% of GDP in 2013).[14]

---

[11] World Bank, "Middle East and North Africa Regional Brief," September 2011, http://go.worldbank.org/1JVC0DGRS0.

[12] World Bank, *Worldwide Governance Indicators*, http://info.worldbank.org/governance/wgi/index.asp.

[13] World Bank, *Doing Business*, 2012, http://www.doingbusiness.org/rankings.

[14] IMF, *World Economic Outlook*, October 2012.

Table 1. Selected Economic Indicators for MENA Countries

	Population	Oil Supply	GDP	GDP per capita	Manufacturing	Services	Unemployment
	Millions	Thousand barrels per day	Billion US$	US$	Value added, % of GDP	Value added, % of GDP	% of total labor force
	2011	2011	2011	2011	Most recent year available since 2008	Most recent year available since 2008	Most recent year available since 2008
Oil exporters							
Algeria	36.0	1,884	189	5,244	5.6[c]	31.0[b]	11.4[b]
Bahrain	1.3	47	23[b]	18,184	–	–	–
Iran	74.8	4,234	331[c]	4,526	–	–	10.5[d]
Iraq	33.0	2,635	115	3,501	–	–	–
Kuwait	2.8	2,682	177	62,664	–	–	–
Libya	6.4	502	62[c]	9,957	4.5[d]	19.9[d]	–
Oman	2.8	889	72	25,221	–	–	–
Qatar	1.9	1,638	173	92,501	–	–	–
Saudi Arabia	28.1	11,153	577	20,540	9.7[b]	37.8[b]	5.4[c]
UAE	7.9	3,088	360	45,653	9.7[b]	43.6[b]	4.0[d]
Yemen	24.8	163	34	1,361	6.1[b]	62.9[b]	14.6[c]
Oil importers							
Djibouti	0.9	0	1[c]	1,203	–	–	–
Egypt	82.5	727	230	2,781	15.2[a]	49.3[a]	9.4
Israel	7.8	4	243	31,282	–	–	6.6[b]
Jordan	6.2	0	29	4,666	19.4[a]	65.6[a]	12.9[c]
Lebanon	4.3	0	42	9,904	8.2[a]	72.4[a]	–
Malta	0.4	0	9	21,209	13.4[b]	65.4[a]	6.9[b]
Morocco	20.8	4	100	3,054	15.5[a]	55.0[a]	10.0[b]
Syria	10.7	331	59[b]	2,893	–	46.5[c]	8.4[c]
Tunisia	4.0	70	46	4,297	17.6[a]	59.7[a]	14.2[d]
West Bank	0.9	0	–	–	–	–	24.5[c]

Source: World Bank, *World Development Indicators*, 2012; U.S. Energy Information Administration, *International Energy Statistics*, 2012.

Note: "–" denotes not available. a. 2011 data; b. 2010 data; c. 2009 data; d. 2008 data.

Weak Integration in the Global Economy

With some exceptions, MENA countries face serious economic challenges despite some countries' large oil and gas production. Weak integration in the global economy, including weak integration within the region, is frequently cited by economists as a factor impeding economic development in the region.

MENA's Trade and Investment with the World

On the surface, MENA appears to be relatively active in global trade. Relative to GDP, the region had the highest level of exports (45% of GDP in 2010) of any major geographic region in the world in that year, and the highest levels of imports (39% of GDP in 2010, see **Figure 3**).[15] Net inflows of foreign direct investment (FDI) into MENA countries were 2.0% of GDP in 2011, slightly below the average for countries worldwide (2.3% of GDP).[16]

Figure 3. MENA's Trade as a Percent of GDP Compared to Other Regions, 2010

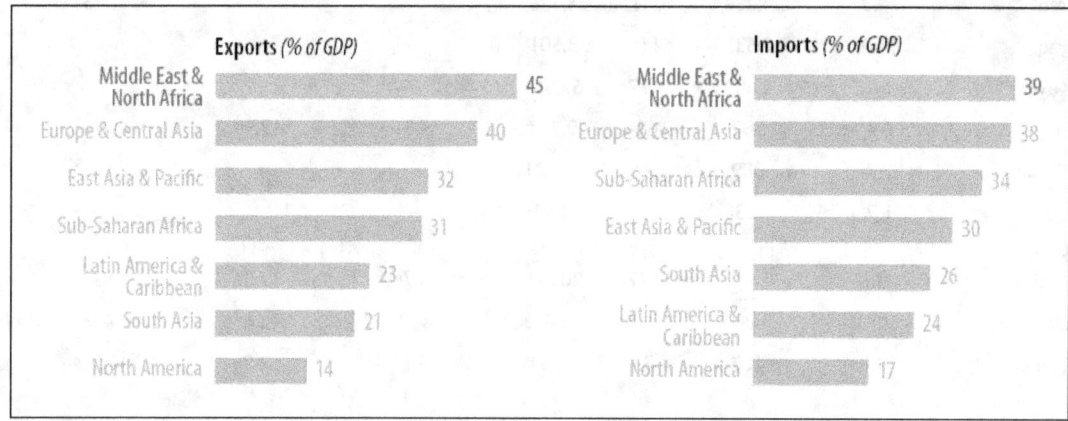

Exports *(% of GDP)*

Middle East & North Africa	45
Europe & Central Asia	40
East Asia & Pacific	32
Sub-Saharan Africa	31
Latin America & Caribbean	23
South Asia	21
North America	14

Imports *(% of GDP)*

Middle East & North Africa	39
Europe & Central Asia	38
Sub-Saharan Africa	34
East Asia & Pacific	30
South Asia	26
Latin America & Caribbean	24
North America	17

Source: World Bank, *World Development Indicators.*

Note: Includes trade in goods and services.

Delving deeper, however, reveals the limitations of MENA's interactions in the global economy. First, MENA's trade tends to be highly concentrated in a few key products. **Figure 4** shows that oil dominates the region's exports, with fuel accounting for 62% of the region's total exports in 2009. MENA's imports are also heavily concentrated on manufactured goods, which accounted for 54% of total imports in 2009, as shown in **Figure 4**.[17] Some lower-income countries in the region still have relatively high levels of protectionism. Tariff rates averaged 6.1% in 2010 among developing MENA countries, compared to an average of 4.3% among developing countries and 2.7% for countries worldwide.[18]

---

[15] World Bank, *World Development Indicators.*

[16] Foreign direct investment (FDI) refers to a company expanding its operations overseas by created a subsidiary, branch, factory, or similar enterprise in a different country. World Bank, *World Development Indicators.*

[17] World Bank, *World Development Indicators.*

[18] World Bank, *World Development Indicators.* Data are for applied tariff rates for all products (weighted mean).

Figure 4. MENA's Exports and Imports of Goods and Services with the World, by Commodity or Type of Service, 2009

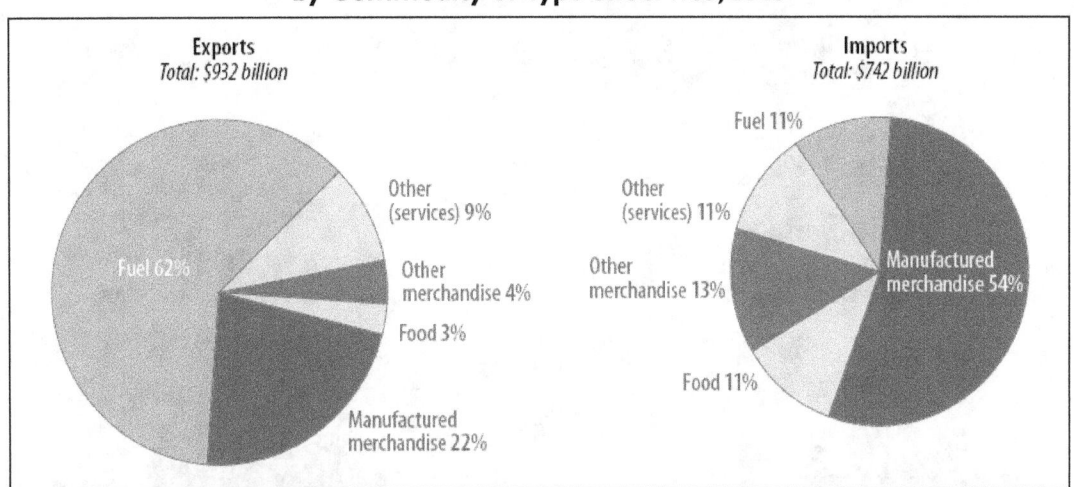

Source: World Bank, *World Development Indicators.*

For trade in goods, MENA's biggest trading partner is the European Union (EU), although countries in the region also trade heavily with Japan, the United States, and large emerging markets, including China and India, as shown in **Figure 5**.[19] Intra-MENA trade is relatively limited, accounting for just 10% of total exports and 16% of total imports in 2011.[20]

There are a number of economic and political explanations for why trade within the region is limited. Some of the countries in the region produce similar products, limiting the opportunities for intra-regional trade. Political tensions among countries also may restrict intra-regional trade. For example, the Arab League, an umbrella organization of more than 20 Middle Eastern and African countries and entities, has maintained an official boycott of Israeli companies and Israeli-made goods since the founding of Israel in 1948.[21]

---

[19] IMF, *Direction of Trade Statistics*.

[20] Ibid.

[21] For more on the Arab League, see CRS Report RL33961, *Arab League Boycott of Israel*, by Martin A. Weiss.

Figure 5. MENA's Major Trading Partners, 2011

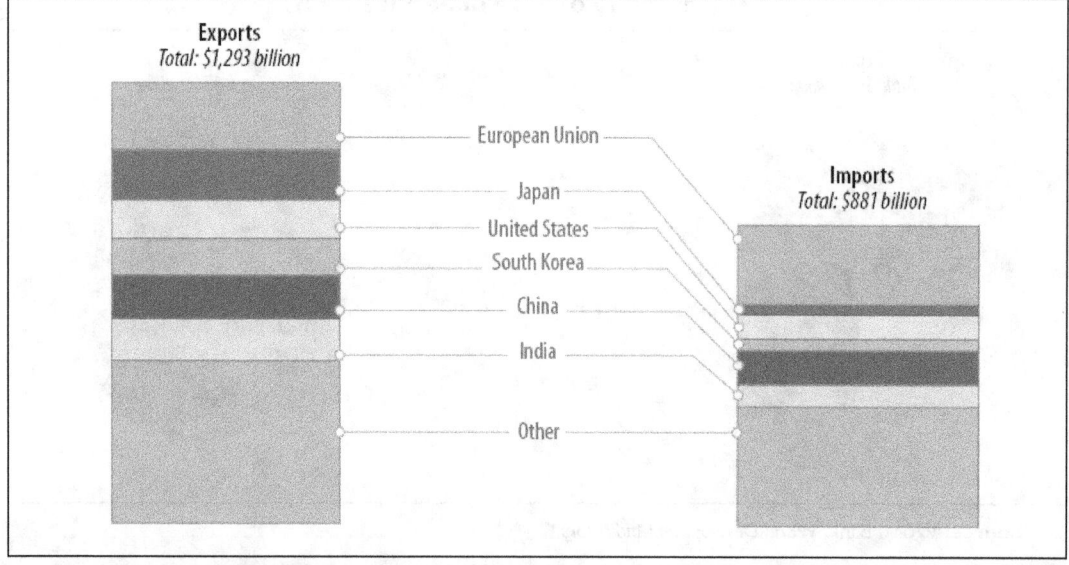

Source: International Monetary Fund (IMF), *Direction of Trade Statistics.*

Notes: Merchandise data only; services data not available.

U.S.-MENA Trade and Investment

Trade

Trade and investment between the MENA and the United States is relatively limited, suggesting scope for deeper economic ties. U.S. trade with MENA countries accounts for a small share of total U.S. trade: $193 billion, about 5% of the U.S. total, in 2011. U.S.-MENA trade primarily consists of exchanging a wide variety of U.S. goods for crude oil, which is then processed and refined into such petroleum end-products as gasoline, diesel fuel, heating oil, kerosene, and liquefied petroleum gas. As shown in **Figure 6**, oil accounted for 73% of all U.S. imports from the MENA in 2011 ($90 billion out of $123 billion). If Israel was removed from the list of countries, oil's share of all U.S. imports from the region would rise to over 90%. Despite the fact that the MENA consists of several oil exporters, it still ranks as the second largest U.S. oil supplier, accounting for about one-fifth (21%) of U.S. oil imports, with Canada ranking first (24%) and Mexico third (10%). The United States exports a range of goods to the MENA region, including motor vehicles, machinery, aircrafts, and diamonds (**Figure 6**).

Figure 6. Top U.S. Exports to and Imports from the MENA Region, 2011

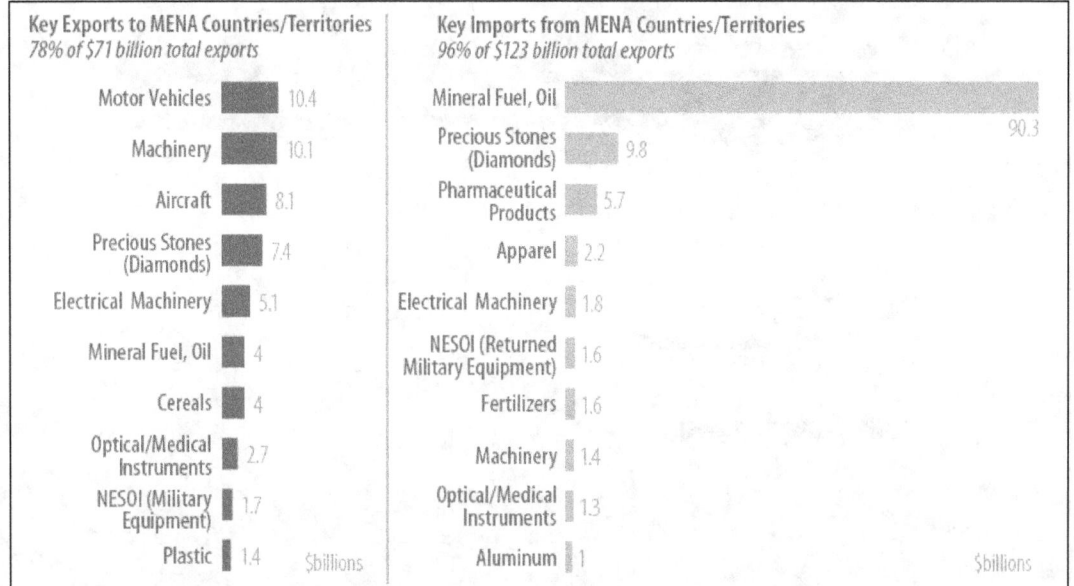

Source: USITC Dataweb--total exports and general imports.

Notes: NEOSI = Not elsewhere specified or included. See the **Appendix** for more detailed data.

Within the region, the value of U.S. trade with individual economies varies widely (**Figure 7**). In 2011, U.S. trade with the MENA region was concentrated in eight countries: Saudi Arabia, Israel, Algeria, Iraq, UAE, Egypt, Kuwait, and Qatar. Together, these eight countries accounted for more than 90% of all U.S. trade (exports and imports) with the region. For four of these countries— Saudi Arabia, Algeria, Iraq, and Kuwait, (designated by a red dot in **Figure 7**)—oil constituted nearly all of their exports to the United States. Other countries for which oil represents more than 65% of its exports included Qatar, Oman, Tunisia, Yemen, Libya, and Syria. In contrast, Israel exports a broader mix of products to the United States. More detailed trade data are provided in the **Appendix**.

Figure 7. U.S. Exports to and Imports from MENA Countries/Territories, 2011

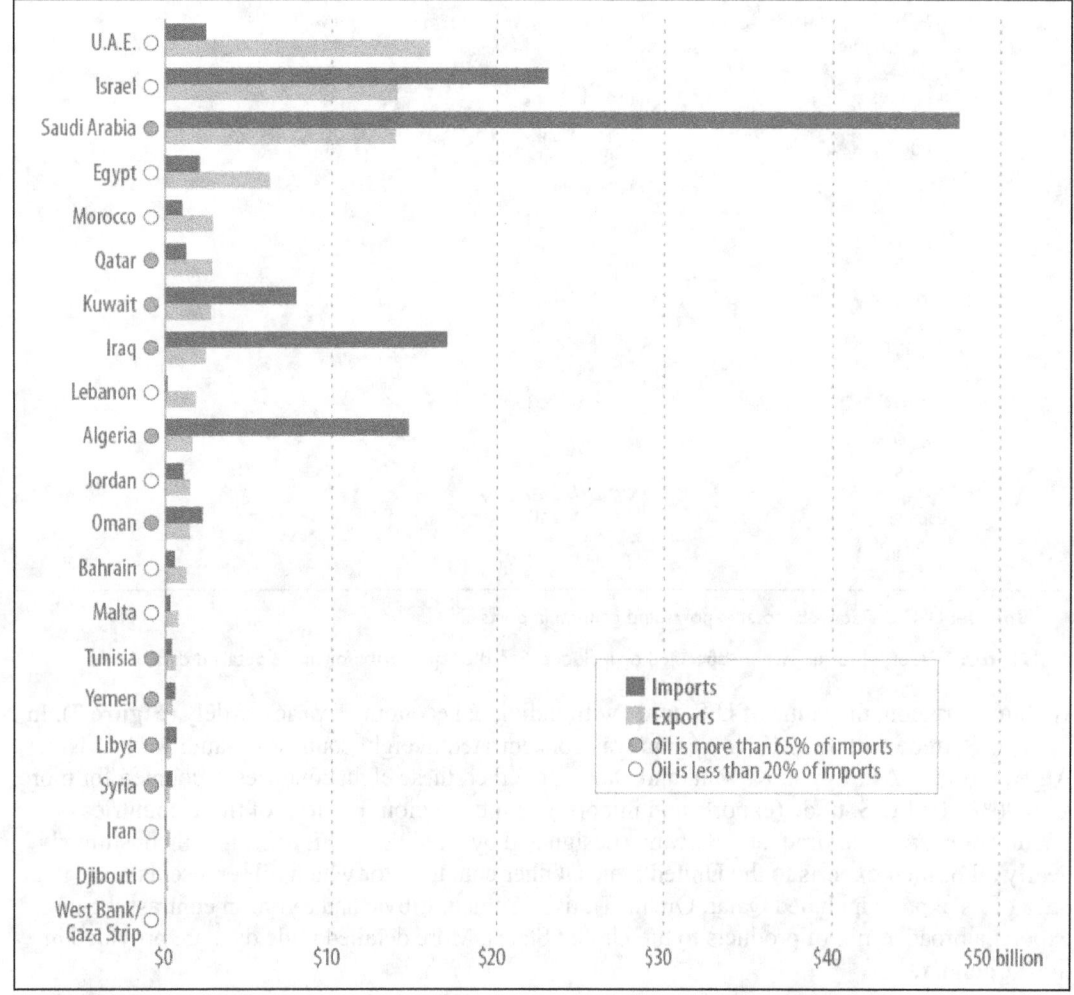

Source: Global Trade Atlas.

Note: U.S. exports to MENA total $71 billion; and imports total $123 billion. See the **Appendix** for more detailed data.

Foreign Direct Investment (FDI)

Closely linked to trade is FDI. **Figure 8** shows that the MENA region accounts for a small share of global FDI by U.S. firms ("outward" FDI). In 2011, the total stock of U.S. outward FDI was $4.2 trillion.[22] Of this, about only $56 billion, or 1%, was invested in the MENA region.[23]

---

[22] FDI data are from the Department of Commerce, Bureau of Economic Analysis (BEA). BEA defines FDI as a business enterprise that is owned 10% or more, directly or indirectly, by a foreign person or company.

[23] Includes FDI from the United States to Algeria, Bahrain, Djibouti, Egypt, Iran, Iraq, Israel, Jordan, Kuwait, Lebanon, Libya, Morocco, Oman, Qatar, Saudi Arabia, Syria, Tunisia, UAE, and Yemen. Uniworld, a privately held publishing firm, maintains a database on overseas investments by private firms. Its listings show that many of the investors in the MENA countries/territories are familiar U.S. corporations, including Starbucks, Pitney Bowes, Polo Ralph Lauren, Sodexo, Coca-Cola, Hertz, Ritz Carlton, Tupperware, UPS, W.R. Grace & Company, Wachovia, 3M, (continued...)

Likewise, the total stock of FDI in the United States ("inward" FDI), in 2011 was $2.5 trillion. Firms located in MENA countries accounted for approximately $17 billion, or 1% of total FDI into the United States.[24]

Figure 8. U.S.-MENA Foreign Direct Investment (FDI), 2011

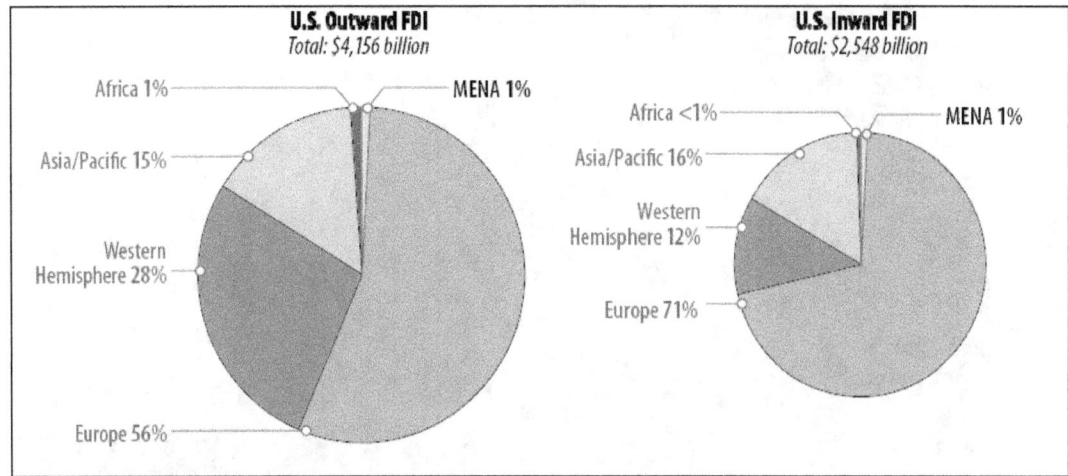

Source: Department of Commerce, Bureau of Economic Analysis (BEA).

Notes: BEA classification of countries by region, with the exception of Egypt, Algeria, Djibouti, Libya, Morocco, and Tunisia re-classified to be in the MENA region rather than the African region. U.S. "outward" FDI refers to U.S. FDI into MENA countries/territories. U.S. "inward" FDI refers to FDI flowing from MENA countries/territories to the United States. Data are for the stock of FDI, rather than flows of FDI, and are on a historical-cost basis.

Figure 9 shows the stock of U.S. foreign direct investment in specific MENA economies in 2011. FDI from the United States to the region was concentrated in a small number of countries, including Egypt, Qatar, Israel, Saudi Arabia, Algeria, and the UAE. **Figure 9** also shows that Israel accounted for roughly 90% of FDI into the United States from MENA countries, with more than $15 billion invested in the United States.

(...continued)

Century 21, Curves, Dale Carnegie, Hewlett Packard, Johnson & Johnson, McDonalds, Microsoft, Motorola, Office Depot, Dun & Bradstreet, Estee Lauder, and Xerox, as well as numerous oil and drilling companies including Chevron, Exxon Mobil, Conoco Phillips, Occidental Petroleum, and Schlumberger.

[24] Includes FDI to the United States from Bahrain, Egypt, Iran, Iraq, Israel, Jordan, Kuwait, Lebanon, Libya, Morocco, Oman, Qatar, Saudi Arabia, Syria, UAE, and Yemen.

Figure 9. U.S.-MENA Foreign Direct Investment (FDI): Country Breakdown, 2011

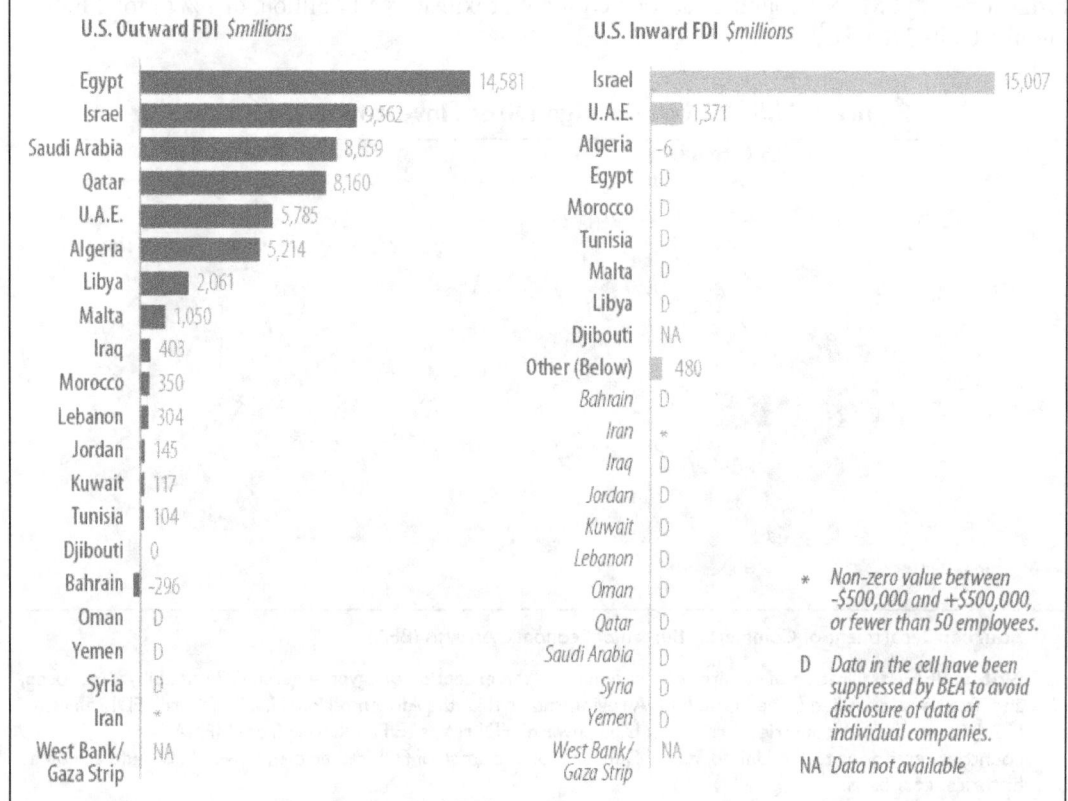

Source: U.S. Department of Commerce, Bureau of Economic Analysis (BEA).

Notes: U.S. "outward" FDI refers to U.S. FDI into MENA countries/territories, and totaled $56 billion in 2011. U.S. "inward" FDI refers to FDI flowing from MENA countries/territories to the United States, and totaled $17 billion in 2011. Data are for the stock of FDI, rather than flows of FDI. Data are on a historical-cost basis. Note that for inward flows to the United States, "other" includes Bahrain, Iran, Iraq, Jordan, Kuwait, Lebanon, Oman, Qatar, Saudi Arabia, Syria, and Yemen.

• Negative positions can occur when a parent company's liabilities to the foreign affiliate are greater than its equity in and loans to the foreign affiliate.

Obstacles to Closer U.S. Trade and Investment Ties with MENA Countries

What factors have limited U.S.-MENA trade and investment ties? Some countries in the region have undertaken efforts to improve their regulatory and business environments. However, serious challenges remain to international firms, including U.S. firms, looking to do business in the region. One source of information about obstacles to doing business in various countries overseas is the *Country Commercial Guides* published by the U.S. Commercial Service, part of the Department of Commerce.[25] For the region, the reports generally emphasize impediments to U.S. firms seeking to do business in MENA countries related to lack of transparency, bureaucratic red

---

[25] The *Country Commercial Guides* are available at http://export.gov/worldwide_us/index.asp. The State Department's *Investment Climate Statements* are included as part of the FCS's *Country Commercial Guides*. The State Department publishes their *Investment Climate Statements* on their website at http://www.state.gov/e/eeb/rls/othr/ics/.

tape, weak rule of law, corruption, and differences in business cultures. Some examples of issues raised by these U.S. government reports in selected MENA countries are listed below.

- **Egypt:** corruption; ill-defined regulatory framework; generally unresponsive commercial court system; and multiplicity of regulations and regulatory agencies.[26]

- **Tunisia:** inconsistent procedures in customs administration and delays in customs clearance.[27]

- **Morocco:** irregularities and lack of transparency in government procurement procedures; corruption; and counterfeit goods.[28]

- **Saudi Arabia:** weak enforcement of arbitration of private sector disputes; foreign visitors need to obtain a local sponsor to obtain a business visa; and preference to local firms in government contracts.[29]

- **UAE:** difficult to dismiss non-performing local employees; difficult to sell without a local partner; slow payments; and cumbersome dispute resolution mechanisms.[30]

U.S. Trade and Investment Policy with MENA

Given the economic and governance challenges, recent political upheaval, and the MENA region's limited integration into world markets, policymakers, both domestically and internationally, have discussed how trade and investment could foster support for successful and stable democratic transitions. For example, President Obama said in his May 2011 speech on the region that, "just as democratic revolutions can be triggered by a lack of individual opportunity, successful democratic transitions depend upon an expansion of growth and broad-based prosperity."[31]

U.S. trade policy in the region is focused on using trade and investment to foster economic growth, promote greater economic reforms, provide support for successful and stable democratic transitions, and generally support U.S. foreign policy objectives. Such goals also fit into longstanding and overall U.S. trade policy goals of creating and sustaining U.S. jobs by opening

---

[26] U.S. Commercial Service, "Doing Business in Egypt: 2012 Country Commercial Guide for U.S. Companies," http://www.buyusainfo.net/docs/x_8534139.pdf.

[27] U.S. Commercial Service, "Doing Business in Tunisia: 2012 Country Commercial Guide for U.S. Companies," http://photos.state.gov/libraries/tunisia/231771/PDFs/2012%20Tunisia%20Country%20Commercial%20Guide.pdf.

[28] U.S. Commercial Service, "Doing Business in Morocco: 2011 Country Commercial Guide for U.S. Companies," http://www.buyusainfo.net/docs/x_1606158.pdf.

[29] U.S. Commercial Service, "Doing Business in Saudi Arabia: 2011 Country Commercial Guide for U.S. Companies," http://export.gov/saudiarabia/static/CCG_Latest_eg_sa_056382.pdf.

[30] U.S. Commercial Service, "Doing Business in the United Arab Emirates: 2012 Country Commercial Guide for U.S. Companies," http://export.gov/unitedarabemirates/build/groups/public/@eg_ae/documents/webcontent/eg_ae_052507.pdf.

[31] Office of the Press Secretary, "Remarks by the President on the Middle East and North Africa," The White House, State Department, Washington, DC, May 19, 2011, http://www.whitehouse.gov/the-press-office/2011/05/19/remarks-president-middle-east-and-north-africa.

---

international markets and through rules-based trade, as well as by monitoring and enforcing U.S. rights under trade agreements.

Important exceptions to overall U.S. trade policy objectives in the region are Iran and Syria. There is broad international support, including from the United States, to support progressively strict economic sanctions on Iran to try to compel it to verifiably confine its nuclear program to purely peaceful uses.[32] Likewise, the State Department has designated Syria as a state sponsor of terrorism, making Syria subject to a number of legislatively mandated penalties, including export sanctions and ineligibility to receive most forms of U.S. aid or to purchase U.S. military equipment.[33] Should fundamental political change occur in Syria, Congress may revisit longstanding restrictions in consultation with the Administration.

Overview of U.S. Trade Policy Tools

The United States uses policy tools to promote trade and investment, both with the MENA and globally, that may be grouped into two broad categories: (1) formal agreements and discussion frameworks to liberalize trade and investment and advance rules-based trade, such as free trade agreements and bilateral investment treaties; and (2) U.S. federal government programs that aim to encourage international trade and investment, such as export assistance and financing. Details on selected policy tools are provided in the text box below.

---

[32] For more on Iran sanctions, see CRS Report RS20871, *Iran Sanctions*, by Kenneth Katzman.

[33] State Department, "Background Note: Syria," March 18, 2011, http://www.state.gov/r/pa/ei/bgn/3580.htm; CRS Report RL33487, *Armed Conflict in Syria: U.S. and International Response*, by Jeremy M. Sharp and Christopher M. Blanchard.

Background on Selected U.S. Trade and Investment Policy Tools

Multilateral Trade Agreements

- The **World Trade Organization (WTO)** is a multilateral body that establishes liberalized and rules-based trade through negotiations; implements a rules-based system for trade in goods and services and other trade-related matters; and adjudicates disputes under the rules. Accession to the WTO includes implementation of WTO agreements, the establishment of stable and predictable market access for goods and services, and the development of a proven framework for adopting policies and practices that promote trade, investment, growth, and development. The WTO has 159 members.

Bilateral Trade and Investment Discussions

- **Trade and Investment Frameworks (TIFAs)** are agreements between the United States and another country or a group of countries to consult on issues of mutual interest in order to facilitate trade and investment. TIFAs are non-binding, do not involve changes to U.S. law, and therefore, do not require congressional approval. TIFAs may lead to free trade agreement negotiations (see below).

Bilateral Trade and Investment Agreements

- **Free Trade Agreements (FTAs)** are reciprocal agreements in which member countries agree to eliminate tariff and non-tariff barriers on trade in goods, services, and agriculture between or among countries covered by the agreement, and to establish rules in trade-related areas, such as investment, intellectual property rights (IPR), labor, and the environment. FTAs also can enhance and "lock in" domestic economic reform in partner countries, such as on transparency of regulatory policies, IPR protection, and customs procedures. U.S. FTAs generally are comprehensive and "high-standard" agreements and, in certain cases, go beyond WTO commitments. Congress must approve implementing legislation for FTAs in order for U.S. commitments under the agreements to enter into force. The United States has entered into 14 FTAs with 20 countries.

- **Bilateral Investment Treaties (BITs)** establish binding rules for the reciprocal protection of investment in each other's territories. Most BITs contain provisions that assure U.S. and foreign partner country investors of non-discriminatory treatment of investments by the host country, place limits on expropriation of investments, and provide for due process to settle investment-related disputes with host governments, among other things. As treaties, U.S. BITs are ratified by the Senate. The United States has 41 BITs in-force.

U.S. Federal Government Programs to Encourage Trade and Investment

- **Export promotion** constitutes a wide variety of functions that may directly or indirectly support the expansion of U.S. exports, including providing information, counseling, and export assistance services; funding feasibility studies; financing and insuring U.S. trade; conducting government-to-government advocacy; and negotiating new trade agreements and enforcing existing ones. Congress authorizes and provides appropriations for export promotion-related programs.

- **Trade preference programs** provide preferential treatment, usually in the form of lower tariffs or duty-free treatment, to a range of imports from eligible developing countries to promote their economic development and growth by stimulating exports and investment. Congress authorizes trade preference programs. The **Generalized System of Preferences (GSP)** is the most comprehensive of all U.S. trade preference programs. Specifically, GSP provides non-reciprocal, duty-free tariff treatment to certain products imported from designated beneficiary developing countries. Certain "import sensitive" products are specifically excluded from preferential treatment. These include most textile and apparel goods, watches, footwear and other accessories, most electronics, steel and glass products, and certain agricultural products subject to tariff-rate quotas.

- **Qualifying Industrial Zones (QIZs)**, established by Congress in 1996, permit Jordan and Egypt to export duty-free certain products manufactured in designated zones in their countries to the United States, provided that they contain a certain percentage of inputs from their respective countries and from Israel.

Note: Congress has oversight, authorization, and appropriation responsibilities related to U.S. trade and investment policies and programs.

MENA Trade and Investment Partnership Initiative

The U.S. government has organized much of its trade policy response to the political change in the region through the MENA "Trade and Investment Partnership" (MENA-TIP). Announced by President Obama in May 2011, the objectives of the initiative are to facilitate trade within the region; promote greater trade and investment with the United States and with other global markets; and "open the door to willing and able MENA partners—particularly those adopting high standards of reform and trade liberalization—to construct a regional trade arrangement."[34] Under this initiative, the United States has engaged primarily with Egypt, Jordan, Morocco, and Tunisia, focusing cooperation initially on investment, trade facilitation, support for small- and medium-sized enterprises (SMEs), and regulatory practices and transparency.[35] The United States also has engaged, to a lesser extent, with Libya.

The Office of the U.S. Trade Representative (USTR), which formulates, coordinates, and implements U.S. trade policy, takes the lead on implementing the MENA-TIP initiative. Other government agencies, including the Departments of Commerce, State, and the Treasury, also participate in the initiative.

Efforts under the MENA-TIP initiative include:

- **Egypt:** In January 2012, the United States and Egypt announced their intention to develop an "Action Plan" to enhance the bilateral trade relationship. The two sides have outlined possible steps to achieve objectives in three main areas. Actions to: (1) *boost exports* could include enhancing Egypt's utilization of the Generalized System of Preferences and Qualifying Industrial Zones programs; (2) *promote investment* could include business missions and investment conferences, the development of a joint statement on investment and services, and technical assistance; and (3) *strengthen Egypt's SME sector* could include sharing best practices, establishing SME business centers in Egypt, and providing Overseas Private Investment Corporation financing to encourage lending by Egyptian banks to Egyptian small businesses.[36]

- **Morocco:** In December 2012, the United States announced the completion of two bilateral agreements with Morocco to stimulate bilateral and regional trade and investment. The non-binding "Joint Principles for International Investment" is intended to signal commitment to adopt and maintain an open, stable investment environment. Similarly, the non-binding "Joint Principles for Information and Communication Technology (ICT) Services" is intended to demonstrate commitment to the global

---

[34] Office of the Press Secretary, "Remarks by the President on the Middle East and North Africa," The White House, State Department, Washington, DC, May 19, 2011, http://www.whitehouse.gov/the-press-office/2011/05/19/remarks-president-middle-east-and-north-africa. Office of the United States Trade Representative (USTR), "Remarks by Ambassador Miriam Sapiro on Trade and Investment with the Middle East and North Africa," press release, September 15, 2011, http://www.ustr.gov/about-us/press-office/speeches/transcripts/2011/september/remarks-ambassador-miriam-sapiro-trade.

[35] USTR, "Agreed Summary: Initial Meeting on Building a New Trade & Investment Partnership," press release, April 2012, http://www.ustr.gov/webfm_send/3348.

[36] USTR, "Egypt-U.S. Trade and Investment Partnership Promotion Opportunity & Job Creation," January 2012, http://www.ustr.gov/about-us/press-office/press-releases/2012/january/egypt---us-trade-and-investment-partnership-promot.

---

development of ICT services. Both sets of principles are modeled after U.S.-EU agreements. The United States and Morocco also are discussing a third, possibly binding agreement on trade facilitation, modeled after negotiations in the World Trade Organization. The agreement could include new commitments reflecting electronic and other developments in trade facilitation since the U.S.-Morocco free trade agreement (FTA) was signed in 2004.[37]

- **Jordan:** In January 2013, the United States announced the completion of two bilateral agreements with Jordan, a "Joint Principles for International Investment" and "Joint Principles for Information and Communications Technology (ICT) Services." These agreements are the same as the December 2012 agreements signed between the United States and Morocco (discussed above). In addition, the United States and Jordan concluded an "Implementation Plan Related to Working and Living Conditions of Workers," which reaffirms Jordan's commitment to protect internationally recognized worker rights and to enforce its labor laws. Follow-up cooperation on labor issues is planned, including through the Labor Subcommittee established as part of the U.S.-Jordan FTA.[38]

The United States may negotiate similar sets of agreements on principles with other countries in the region, such as Egypt.[39]

Formal Agreements and Discussion Frameworks to Liberalize Trade and Investment

Current U.S. trade and investment initiatives with MENA countries are the result of previous efforts undertaken to expand economic and political ties with the region. The Bush Administration in 2003 launched a plan to create a U.S. Middle East Free Trade Area (MEFTA) by 2013. MEFTA aimed to support economic growth and prosperity in the Middle East through liberalizing trade and investment regionally and bilaterally with the United States, as part of a broader plan to fight terrorism. The plan included actively supporting membership in the World Trade Organization (WTO) for countries in the region who were not yet members, negotiating formal bilateral investment treaties (BITs) with interested countries, and negotiating comprehensive free trade agreements (FTAs), among other provisions. The initiative, carried out over several years, fell short of creating a regional free trade area, but did result in the completion of new FTAs with four countries in the region: Bahrain, Jordan, Morocco, and Oman. FTAs were also explored with the UAE and Egypt. Before MEFTA, the only FTA that the United States had in the region was with Israel, completed in 1985.

The United States currently has a network of trade and investment agreements in the MENA region that vary dramatically across countries (**Table 2**). Most of the countries in the region are

---

[37] USTR, "United States and Morocco Reach Agreement on Trade Facilitation, Joint Investment Principles and Joint Information and Communication Technology (ICT) Principles," press release, December 7, 2012, http://www.ustr.gov/about-us/press-office/press-releases/2012/december/us-morocco-reach-agreement.

[38] USTR, "U.S. Trade Representative Ron Kirk Announces Agreements Between the United States and Jordan to Boost Investment and Economic Growth, Enhance Labor Cooperation," press release, January 28, 2013, http://www.ustr.gov/about-us/press-office/press-releases/2013/january/ustr-kirk-announces-us-jordan-agreements. Electronic communication with USTR official, January 30, 2013.

[39] Meeting with USTR officials, January 10, 2013.

members of the WTO. The MENA countries that are not—Algeria, Iran, Iraq, Lebanon, Libya, Syria, and Yemen—have "observer status," which enables them to follow discussions on matters of direct interest to them. With the exception of Syria, all of these countries are in various stages of the process to join the WTO.[40] The United States has supported some of these efforts, for example, providing technical support to Iraq, Lebanon, and Yemen for their WTO accession efforts.[41]

Presently, the United States has Trade and Investment Framework Agreements (TIFAs) with most MENA countries, and bilateral investment treaties (BITs) with five MENA countries: Bahrain, Egypt, Jordan, Morocco, and Tunisia. It also has FTAs with five countries in the region: Bahrain, Israel, Jordan, Morocco, and Oman. U.S. FTA negotiations with some MENA countries have experienced complications. For example, discussions on a potential FTA between the United States and Egypt were put on hold in 2005 due to concerns over election results and human rights. Issues of particular concern included questions about Egypt's willingness to negotiate a comprehensive FTA, the adequacy of Egypt's intellectual property rights regime, and import duties for certain apparel and textile products.[42] As another example, negotiations between the United States and the UAE on an FTA were placed on hold in 2007, complicated by differing views on issues related to labor, market access for services, and government procurement.

Elements of this network of trade agreements and policy initiatives serve as additional components of U.S. economic engagement with the MENA. For instance, in support of Tunisia's political transition, in October 2011, the United States and Tunisia "re-launched" talks under the TIFA, originally established in 2002.[43] In March 2012, they met under the bilateral TIFA Council to explore options for bolstering bilateral and intra-regional trade and investment ties.[44] The United States also seeks to enforce U.S. rights under existing trade and investment agreements with MENA countries.

---

[40] See World Trade Organization (WTO), "Accessions," http://www.wto.org/english/thewto_e/acc_e/acc_e.htm.

[41] USTR, *2012 Trade Policy Agenda and 2011 Annual Report*, Annex II, http://www.ustr.gov/about-us/press-office/reports-and-publications/2012-0.

[42] Barbara Kotschwar and Jeffrey J. Schott, *Reengaging Egypt: Options for US-Egypt Economic Relations*, Peterson Institute for International Economics, January 2010.

[43] USTR, "United States and Tunisia Re-Launch Bilateral Trade and Investment Talks in Support of Tunisia's Democratic Transition," press release, October 2011, http://www.ustr.gov/about-us/press-office/press-releases/2011/october/united-states-and-tunisia-re-launch-bilateral-trad.

[44] USTR, "United States and Tunisia Discuss New Approaches to Foster Trade and Investment," March 2012, http://www.ustr.gov/about-us/press-office/press-releases/2012/march/united-states-and-tunisia-discuss-new-approaches-fos.

Table 2. U.S.-MENA Trade and Investment Agreements

	WTO membership (year joined)[a]	Generalized System of Preferences[b]	Trade and Investment Framework Agreements (year signed)	Bilateral Investment Treaty with the United States (year entered into force)	Bilateral Free Trade Agreement with the United States (year entered into force)
Algeria	(Observer)	√	√ 2001		
Bahrain	√ 1995		√ 2002	√ 2001	√ 2006
Djibouti	√ 1995	√			
Egypt	√ 1995	√	√ 1999	√ 1992	
Iran	(Observer)				
Iraq	(Observer)	√	√ 2005		
Israel	√ 1995				√ 1985
Jordan	√ 2000	√		√ 2003	√ 2010
Kuwait	√ 1995		√ 2004		
Lebanon	(Observer)	√	√ 2006		
Libya	(Observer)		√ 2010		
Malta	√ 1995				
Morocco	√ 1995			√ 1991[c]	√ 2006
Oman	√ 2000	√	√ 2004		√ 2009[d]
Qatar	√ 1996		√ 2004		
Saudi Arabia	√ 2005		√ 2003		
Syria	(Observer)				
Tunisia	√ 1995	√	√ 2002	√ 1993	
United Arab Emirates	√ 1996		√ 2004		
West Bank / Gaza Strip		√			
Yemen	(Observer)	√	√ 2004		

Source: CRS Report RL32638, *Middle East Free Trade Area: Progress Report*, by Mary Jane Bolle; CRS Report RL33663, *Generalized System of Preferences: Background and Renewal Debate*, by Vivian C. Jones.

Notes: Countries listed are based on the World Bank's classification of countries in the region (excluding West Bank).

a. The purpose of observer status for international intergovernmental organizations in the WTO is to enable these organizations to follow discussions therein on matters of direct interest to them.

b. Based on Generalized System of Preferences (GSP) eligibility criteria, some countries on the table are ineligible for GSP because, for example, they are developed (e.g., Bahrain, Israel, UAE) or are designated as state sponsors of terrorism (e.g., Iran, Syria).

c. FTA includes investment chapters with updated investment provisions.

d. FTA includes investment chapter modeled after BIT provisions.

Other Federal Programs to Promote Trade and Investment

In addition to formal agreements to liberalize trade and investment and advance rules-based trade, the United States relies on federal programs to encourage and support international trade and investment. For the MENA countries, the most important of these programs include the Generalized System of Preferences (GSP); Qualifying Industrial Zones (QIZ); and export finance and other export promotion programs run by various federal government agencies. Certain elements of such programs are a part of the MENA-TIP Initiative.

Generalized System of Preferences (GSP)

The United States grants preferential treatment to imports from certain developing countries under the GSP program.[45] GSP beneficiary countries in MENA include Algeria, Djibouti, Egypt, Iraq, Jordan, Lebanon, Oman, Tunisia, the West Bank/Gaza Strip, and Yemen. Specifically, GSP allows certain products from designated developing countries to enter the United States duty-free. In order to be eligible for GSP, countries must comply with trade, investment, labor, and other conditions.[46] The United States first authorized the program in 1974. In October 2011, President Obama signed legislation authorizing GSP through July 31, 2013 (P.L. 112-40).

Overall, GSP program utilization among beneficiary developing countries, including in the MENA region, remains low. In 2011, 0.8% of total U.S. imports from beneficiary developing countries in the MENA constituted goods entering the United States under GSP.[47] One reason for this is that oil accounts for more than 70% of all MENA exports to the United States, but oil from most MENA countries is not eligible for GSP tariff benefits. Additionally, some of the region's other major exports, including apparel, iron, and steel, are goods that are excluded from preferential treatment under the GSP program.

Qualifying Industrial Zones (QIZs)

QIZs, established by Congress in 1996, permit the West Bank, the Gaza Strip, and qualifying zones in Egypt and Jordan to export certain products to the United States duty-free.[48] Products eligible for duty-free export to the United States must be manufactured in the West Bank, the Gaza Strip, or specified designated zones within Jordan or Egypt and must contain a certain percentage of inputs from Israel. The purpose of the QIZ legislation is to support the Middle East peace process and to build closer economic ties between Israel and its Arab neighbors. U.S. imports under the QIZ programs in both Egypt and Jordan are dominated by apparel products.

- **Jordan:** Exports from Jordan to the United States under the QIZ program grew from about $159,000 in 1999 to about $95 million in 2011. However, the QIZ share of Jordan's total exports to the United States has declined in recent years,

---

[45] For more information on the GSP program, see CRS Report RL33663, *Generalized System of Preferences: Background and Renewal Debate*, by Vivian C. Jones.

[46] Certain "import sensitive" products are specifically excluded from preferential treatment. These include most textiles and apparel goods, watches, footwear and other accessories, most electronics, steel and glass products, and certain agricultural products subject to tariff-rate quotas.

[47] Ibid.

[48] Section 9 of P.L. 99-47, as amended by P.L. 104-234; 19 USC § 2112 note.

from a high of about 90% in 2002 to about 9% in 2011. This is because most imports from Jordan increasingly enter the United States duty-free under the U.S.-Jordan FTA rather than the QIZ program.

- **Egypt:** Exports from Egypt to the United States under the QIZ program have grown from about $266 million in 2005 to about $1 billion in 2011. The QIZ share of Egypt's total exports to the United States also has grown during this time period, from about 13% in 2005 to about 52% in 2011.[49]

Certain issues have emerged in the QIZ programs. For example, in Jordan's QIZ facilities, labor issues related to working conditions, particularly for migrant laborers, have emerged; the United States is working with Jordan to resolve these issues (see previous discussion on engagement with Jordan under the MENA-TIP initiative).[50]

Government Export Finance and Promotion Programs

The U.S. government plays an active role in promoting U.S. exports of goods and services by administering various forms of export assistance through federal government agencies. A combination of congressional mandates and executive branch actions has directed U.S. export promotion efforts. Most recently, such efforts have been focused through the National Export Initiative (NEI), the Obama Administration's plan to double exports to support U.S. jobs.[51] The NEI does not have a specific emphasis on the MENA, but federal agencies' efforts to boost U.S. exports worldwide under the NEI, such as through more trade missions and greater levels of export financing, may nevertheless contribute to MENA-specific U.S. trade policy goals.

Key export promotion agencies that may play a key role in promoting U.S. commercial ties with MENA countries include the Department of Commerce, Export-Import Bank (Ex-Im Bank), Overseas Private Investment Corporation (OPIC), and Trade and Development Agency (TDA). Taken together, these agencies have representation and/or provide support for U.S. exports and investments for most countries in the region (see **Table 3**). The specific countries in which these agencies provide support may vary according to factors such as their missions, mandated policy criteria, or availability of resources.[52]

---

[49] CRS analysis of data from the USITC, Interactive Tariff and Trade Data Web.

[50] USTR, *2011 Trade Policy Agenda and 2010 Annual Report*. In addition, a 161 page report released by the National Labor Committee in 2006: *U.S.-Jordan Free Trade Agreement Descends into Human Trafficking and Involuntary Servitude*, is a compilation of stories from over 100 guest workers in Jordan.

[51] *Report to the President on the National Export Initiative: The Export Promotion Cabinet's Plan for Doubling U.S. Exports in Five Years*, Washington, D.C., September 2010. Trade Promotion Coordinating Committee (TPCC), *2011 National Export Strategy: Powering the National Export Initiative*, June 2011.

[52] For more information, see CRS Report RL31502, *Nuclear, Biological, Chemical, and Missile Proliferation Sanctions: Selected Current Law*, by Dianne E. Rennack and CRS Report RS20871, *Iran Sanctions*, by Kenneth Katzman.

Table 3. Federal Export and Investment Promotion Support in MENA

Country	Department of Commerce[a] Commercial Service Posts and Representation in-Country	OPIC[b] Availability of Support	TDA[c] Availability of Support	Ex-Im Bank[d] Availability of Support
Algeria	√	√	√	√
Bahrain	*Represented through the State Department "Partner Post"*	√	X	√
Djibouti	X	√	√	√
Egypt	√	√	√	√
Iran	X	X	X	X
Iraq	√	√	√	√
Israel	√	√	X	√
Jordan	√	√	√	√
Kuwait	√	√	X	√
Lebanon	√	√	√	√
Libya	√	X	X	√
Malta	*Represented through the State Department "Partner Post"*	√	X	√
Morocco	√	√	√	√
Oman	*Represented through the State Department "Partner Post"*	√	X	√
Qatar	√	*Suspended (worker rights concerns)*	X	√
Saudi Arabia	√	*Suspended (worker rights concerns)*	X	√
Syria	X	X	X	X
Tunisia	√	√	X	√
United Arab Emirates	√	*Suspended (worker rights concerns)*	X	√
West Bank	√	√	√	√[e]
Yemen	X	√	√	√

Source: Department of Commerce, OPIC, TDA, and Ex-Im Bank agency websites and annual reports; http://www.export.gov; U.S. Government Accountability Office (GAO), *National Export Initiative: U.S. and Foreign Commercial Service Should Improve Performance and Resource Allocation Management*, GAO-11-090, September 2011, p. 57, http://www.gao.gov/new.items/d11909.pdf; and International Trade Administration (ITA) response to CRS inquiry, February 8, 2013.

a. Department of Commerce: A check (√) denotes countries in which there is Commercial Service presence; a cross (X) denotes countries in which the Commercial Service does not have a presence, nor is represented through a "partner post" via the Department of State.

b. OPIC: A check (√) denotes countries in which OPIC support is available; a cross (X) denotes countries in which OPIC support is not available. A list of countries which are eligible for OPIC support is available at http://www.opic.gov/doing-business/investor-screener. OPIC operations were suspended in Qatar, Saudi Arabia, and the UAE in 1995 over concerns about worker rights; see 2013 Investment Climate Statements for the countries (http://www.state.gov/e/eb/rls/othr/ics/2013/index.htm).

c. TDA: A check (√) denotes countries in which TDA support is available; a cross (X) denotes countries in which TDA support is not available. Information on TDA project activity in the MENA region is available at http://www.ustda.gov/program/regions/mena&europe/.

d. Ex-Im Bank: A check (√) denotes countries in which Ex-Im Bank support is available; a cross (X) denotes countries in which Ex-Im Bank support is not available For information on the specific types of Ex-Im Bank financing for which countries are eligible (such as short-term or long-term), see Ex-Im Bank's Country Limitation Schedule: http://www.exim.gov/tools/country/country_limits.cfm.

e. Ex-Im Bank financing for U.S. exports to the West Bank is available, provided that the obligor or guarantor of the transaction is located in a country in which Ex-Im Bank currently has programs available, such as Jordan.

Department of Commerce

The Department of Commerce, through its International Trade Administration (ITA), is the lead agency providing export promotion services for non-agricultural U.S. businesses. With respect to the MENA , ITA's major objectives are to expand U.S. exports, engage in commercial diplomacy (such as through government-to-government advocacy) in support of U.S. business interests, remove market access barriers, and to promote and facilitate inward investment to the United States. ITA's activities include a focus on supporting SMEs in the region. ITA supports USTR's implementation of the MENA-TIP initiative.[53]

The U.S. and Foreign Commercial Service unit of the ITA has a domestic and international network of trade specialists, along with high-level representation at certain U.S. foreign missions, who provide export assistance and advocacy services to U.S. companies seeking foreign business opportunities. The Commercial Service has a presence in many MENA countries (see **Table 3**). At U.S. diplomatic posts where Commercial Service Officers are not present, U.S. Foreign Service Economic Officers of the State Department often conduct U.S. government commercial outreach functions, including through "partnership posts."[54]

Examples of ITA's activity in the region include the following:

- **Trade missions:** In March and April 2011, the Commercial Service led trade missions to Tunisia (focused on investment opportunities); Morocco (energy and port logistics projects); and Saudi Arabia (information technology sector).[55] In 2012, the ITA led a trade mission to Israel (focused on the oil and gas sector). A 2013 trade mission is planned to Egypt and Kuwait, focused on the energy, infrastructure and safety, and security technology sectors.[56]

---

[53] ITA response to CRS inquiry, February 8, 2013.

[54] U.S. Government Accountability Office (GAO), *National Export Initiative: U.S. and Foreign Commercial Service Should Improve Performance and Resource Allocation Management*, GAO-11-909, September 2011, p. 4, http://www.gao.gov/new.items/d11909.pdf.

[55] U.S. Commercial Service, *2011 Annual Report: Powering Export Growth.*

[56] "Trade Mission to Egypt and Kuwait," press release, June 13, 2012, http://export.gov/trademissions/egyptkuwait/.

- **Trade shows:** In January 2013, Commercial Service staff in the UAE supported 200 U.S. exhibitors at the "Arab Health 2013" trade show, the second largest medical equipment sector show in the world.

- **Business development conferences:** ITA assisted in organizing and promoting the first U.S.-Morocco Business Development Conference in December 2012, which included approximately 200 U.S. participants from the private sector.

- **Advocacy:** ITA is working to ensure that U.S. companies can compete for infrastructure projects in Qatar.[57]

Export-Import Bank (Ex-Im Bank)

The Ex-Im Bank provides direct loans, guarantees, and insurance to help finance U.S. exports when the private sector is unable or unwilling to do so, with the goal of contributing to U.S. employment. While MENA is not a specific focus for the agency, Ex-Im Bank authorizations for financing in the region increased markedly between FY2011 and FY2012, from $443 million to $8.9 billion. The share of Ex-Im Bank authorizations for the region also grew, from about 1% in FY2011 (of $32.7 billion in Ex-Im Bank financing worldwide) to about 25% in FY2012 (of $35.8 billion in Ex-Im Bank financing worldwide).

The increase in financing for the region was driven in part by large authorizations to Saudi Arabia, including for U.S. exports for power and petrochemical projects (totaling $5.5 billion in FY2012), and the UAE, for U.S. exports of commercial aircraft and nuclear power plant components and services (totaling $3.3 billion in FY2012).[58]

Overseas Private Investment Corporation (OPIC)

OPIC provides political risk insurance and finance to support U.S. investment in developing countries, which may contribute to U.S. exports and employment. Governed by the Foreign Assistance Act of 1961 (P.L. 87-195), as amended, OPIC's activities are intended to support U.S. foreign policy goals. In FY2011, OPIC committed $108.7 million for new investment projects in MENA countries, close to 4% of OPIC's commitments for new investment projects worldwide in that year ($2.8 billion). The largest destinations for new OPIC commitments in the region were the West Bank and Gaza Strip ($40 million), followed by Iraq ($20.5 million) and Jordan ($3.2 million). In FY2011, OPIC's portfolio exposure in MENA totaled $2.6 billion, close to one-fifth of OPIC's total exposure worldwide in that year ($14.5 billion).[59] OPIC's support in the MENA historically has focused on four key areas: support for SMEs, infrastructure development (including housing, energy, and telecommunications), agriculture and food security, and humanitarian assistance.[60]

---

[57] ITA response to CRS inquiry, February 8, 2013.

[58] Export-Import Bank (Ex-Im Bank) activity levels are based on CRS analysis of data from Ex-Im Bank annual reports, applying the World Bank definition of the MENA region.

[59] Overseas Private Investment Corporation (OPIC) activity levels are based on CRS analysis of data reported in OPIC's FY2011 annual report and FY2013 congressional budget justification. CRS analysis uses the World Bank definition of the MENA region.

[60] OPIC, FY2013 congressional budget justification.

In response to the political change in the region, OPIC has targeted up to $3 billion in support of investment in the region, based on two separate announcements by the Administration:

- In March 2011, Secretary of State Clinton announced that OPIC would provide up to $2 billion in financial support "to catalyze private sector development" in the region to spur economic growth and job creation. Eligible countries include Egypt, Tunisia, Morocco, Iraq, Jordan, Lebanon, and the Palestinian Territories (and potentially Algeria, Oman, and Yemen). The initiative aims to prioritize investments in SMEs, infrastructure (especially renewable resources), and other key sectors. It will also include "fast-track" approval, to ensure "rapid deployment" of capital, while maintaining "OPIC investment policy standards" related to the environment and worker rights.[61]

- In May 2011, President Obama announced that OPIC would provide up to $1 billion in financing to support infrastructure and job creation specifically in Egypt.[62]

Following the 2011 announcements, OPIC approved $500 million in lending to Egypt and Jordan ($250 million to each country) to support small businesses in those countries. Under the facility, OPIC will guarantee loans by local banks in Egypt and Jordan to small businesses, microfinance institutions, non-banking financial institutions, and other approved borrowers. OPIC is collaborating on the loan guarantee facility with the U.S. Agency for International Development (USAID), which will provide grant funding and technical assistance to the initiative.[63] The Egypt loan guarantee facility currently is not operational; the U.S. project sponsors reportedly are awaiting the required permits from the Egyptian government.[64] In comparison, implementation of the Jordan loan guarantee facility reportedly is further along.

Trade and Development Agency (TDA)

TDA, authorized under the Foreign Assistance Act of 1961, as amended, operates under a dual mission of promoting economic development and U.S. commercial interests in developing and middle-income countries. TDA connects U.S. businesses to export opportunities for priority development projects by funding feasibility studies, pilot projects, reverse trade missions, and other activities. In some cases, TDA projects can lead to follow-on financing by OPIC and Ex-Im Bank. The Middle East is one of TDA's major focus areas, and TDA has identified Egypt and Morocco as among 18 "key markets" in which it will focus its programs in FY2013.[65] TDA projects span sectors such as transportation and trade logistics, ICT, energy supply, and water supply management. In FY2012, TDA program funding for the region totaled $5.6 million and constituted about 13% of worldwide TDA funding ($43.9 million), similar to FY2011.[66] Examples of projects include:

---

[61] OPIC, "OPIC to Provide Up to $2 Billion for Investment in Middle East and North Africa," press release, March 11, 2011.

[62] Office of the Press Secretary, "Remarks by the President on the Middle East and North Africa," The White House, State Department, Washington, DC, May 19, 2011, http://www.whitehouse.gov/the-press-office/2011/05/19/remarks-president-middle-east-and-north-africa.

[63] OPIC, "OPIC Board Approves $500 Million for Small Business Lending in Egypt and Jordan," press release, July 1, 2011.

[64] Electronic and telephone communication with CHF International official, January 23, 2013.

[65] Electronic communication with TDA official, February 13, 2013.

[66] Trade and Development Agency (TDA) funding levels are based on CRS analysis of data from TDA annual reports, (continued...)

- In September 2012, TDA concluded two grant agreements to expand Egypt's information communication technology (ICT) infrastructure, one for technical assistance to support implementation of an integrated airport ICT system in Cairo, Egypt ($622,225) and the other for a feasibility study to support building a data center in Katameya, Egypt ($351,000).[67]

- In June 2011, TDA sponsored an *Egypt: Forward* initiative, bringing together 250 U.S. company representatives and 50 Egyptian public and private sector leaders in the energy, ICT, transportation, and agribusiness sectors, in an effort to foster greater commercial and economic ties.[68]

Possible Policy Approaches for Increasing U.S.-MENA Trade and Investment

Government initiatives that foster U.S. private sector trade and investment in MENA countries may be attractive policy options compared to others under discussion, such as debt relief and foreign aid, in a time of tight U.S. budget constraints. They also may provide new opportunities for U.S. businesses overseas and generate stronger economic growth. However, the effects of trade and investment initiatives may be borne out over the long-term, and they may not provide immediate economic relief. A range of potential options—at the unilateral, bilateral/regional, and multilateral levels—are available to Congress, as well as the executive branch, for increasing U.S. trade and investment ties with countries in the MENA region, should there be interest in doing so. This section analyzes policy options for increasing U.S. trade with and investment in MENA economies.

Unilateral Options

Congress could consider a number of unilateral trade policy tools to support and expand U.S. economic relations with countries in transition and other economies in the MENA region. Such policy tools constitute non-reciprocal trade benefits that would not necessarily require negotiations with MENA trading partners, and thus might be easier to implement in the short-term. Countries that receive such trade benefits often have to meet certain criteria (such as worker rights and intellectual property protection requirements) in order to be designated as beneficiaries and to maintain such status. Thus, the U.S. extension of non-reciprocal trade benefits to MENA countries may provide a mechanism to encourage improvement on potential issues of concern.

- **Trade preference programs:** The U.S. government could work with MENA governments to increase their use of existing trade preference programs. For example, under the MENA-TIP initiative, the U.S. government is pursuing efforts

---

(...continued)

applying the World Bank definition of the MENA region. TDA's funding for regional programs are not included in the MENA funding amount because TDA groups the MENA and Europe in one region.

[67] TDA, "USTDA Supporting Expanded ICT Infrastructure in Egypt," press release, September 10, 2012, http://www.ustda.gov/news/pressreleases/2012/MENAEurope/Egypt/EgyptICTInfrastructure_091012.asp.

[68] TDA, *U.S. Trade and Development Agency 2011 Annual Report.* Also, see TDA, *Egypt: Forward,* http://egyptforward.ustda.gov/.

to expand Egypt's utilization of the GSP program. Additionally, Congress could revise provisions of the GSP program to facilitate and expand use by MENA beneficiary countries, such as by expanding product coverage. Such issues could be examined in the context of possible debate in the 113th Congress on extending the authority of the GSP program, which currently expires July 31, 2013.

Congress also could create a regional trade preference program for the MENA region using existing agreements elsewhere as possible models. Currently, Congress has established five regional or targeted trade preference programs: 1) the Andean Trade Preference Program; 2) the Caribbean Basin Economic Recovery Act (CBERA); 3) the Caribbean Trade Partnership Act (CBTPA); 4) the African Growth and Opportunity Act (AGOA); and 5) the Haitian Opportunity through Partnership Encouragement (HOPE) Act.[69]

- **QIZ program:** Congress could consider revising the QIZ program. One option, as currently being discussed by the U.S. and Egyptian governments, could be to expand existing QIZs in Egypt by approving additional zones in these countries.[70] Another option may be to encourage a MENA-wide QIZ, or create QIZs in other countries. Egypt and Jordan were targeted initially for the QIZ program, because they were two Arab countries that had signed peace treaties with Israel. Proposing new Israeli content requirements for QIZ programs may draw criticism from groups opposed to trade with Israel in some MENA countries.

- **Export finance and promotion programs:** Congress could consider boosting U.S. export assistance, financing, and other efforts targeted toward the MENA region, or encouraging the executive branch to do so. For instance, with the end of U.S. combat operations and the formation of a governing political coalition in Iraq, economic development in that country could arguably represent export and investment opportunities for U.S. businesses in areas such as transportation and infrastructure, which could require U.S. export financing and political risk insurance. As another example, assuming the political situation in Libya stabilizes, commercial opportunities may emerge in areas such as energy, housing, and infrastructure. U.S. exporters and investors may benefit from federal assistance in pursuing such opportunities.

Bilateral and Regional Options

Bilateral and regional policy options also may present avenues for congressional efforts to facilitate U.S. trade and investment with MENA partners. Initiatives for trade and investment agreements may be viewed as longer-term policy options, given the timeframes most agreements take to finalize and the readiness of trading partners to negotiate specific commitments. However, the broader scope of most agreements creates opportunities to affect multiple sectors, foster important economic and governance reforms, and support greater regional integration. To reduce

---

[69] For more information on the role of Congress in establishing these programs, see CRS Report R41429, *Trade Preferences: Economic Issues and Policy Options*, coordinated by Vivian C. Jones.

[70] Department of State, "Joint Statement on Egypt-U.S. Trade and Investment Partnership," press release, January 27, 2012, http://iipdigital.usembassy.gov/st/english/texttrans/2012/01/20120127173834su0.2903057.html#axzz2KcXIiB1Q.

---

and eliminate tariff and non-tariff barriers to U.S. exports, trade negotiations would allow the United States to gain greater market access to MENA countries, which could assuage U.S. political opposition from import-sensitive sectors of the economy.[71] On the other hand, increased U.S. and other foreign import penetration of regional economies may be opposed by regional economic actors seeking protection from international competitors. In the past, Middle East countries have pursued FTAs with the United States in part to help lock in and advance domestic economic reforms and diversify their economies by building economic ties with the United States, among other objectives.

- **Launching and re-launching TIFAs:** The United States has TIFAs with most "developing countries" in the MENA region, Iran and Syria notwithstanding. In 2011, the United States re-launched discussions under the 2002 TIFA with Tunisia to support bilateral trade and investment and regional economic integration.[72] In the same vein, the United States could re-launch TIFAs with other MENA countries. One candidate could be Egypt, in order to reinvigorate potential FTA discussions, although it is worth noting that the United States and Egypt conduct trade and economic dialogues through other mechanisms as well.[73]

  Negotiating new trade and investment agreements, bilaterally or regionally: Longer-term, the United States could choose to focus its negotiations on trade and investment agreements with selected countries currently undergoing political transitions, such as Egypt or Tunisia. According to some experts, expanding the U.S. partnership with Egypt through an FTA could help to promote economic development, support political reform, contribute to rising living standards for Egyptians, and serve as an incentive for Egypt to play a constructive role in the region and strengthen its ties with economic partners.[74] An FTA with Egypt could also potentially advance other reforms, such as those related to transparency, governance, regulatory standards, and privatization that support economic growth more broadly.[75] However, it is worth noting that under a potential U.S.-Egypt FTA, economic benefits of greater trade and investment for Egypt likely would occur in the longer-term; they would not necessarily help to directly address Egypt's short-term economic problems, such as pressures on the country's public debt. In addition, there is concern that, unless complementary reforms are undertaken, the benefits of an FTA may be limited to a narrow section of

---

[71] Andrew H. Card and Thomas A. Daschle, Chairs and Edward Alden and Matthew J. Slaughter, Project Directors, *U.S. Trade and Investment Policy*, Council on Foreign Relations, Independent Task Force Report No. 67, 2011.

[72] USTR, "United States and Tunisia Re-Launch Bilateral Trade and Investment Talks in Support of Tunisia's Democratic Transition," press release, October 2011, http://www.ustr.gov/about-us/press-office/press-releases/2011/october/united-states-and-tunisia-re-launch-bilateral-trad.

[73] USTR, "United States and Egypt Advance Bilateral Trade and Investment Talks in Support of Egypt's Democratic Transition," press release, October 2011, http://www.ustr.gov/about-us/press-office/press-releases/2011/october/united-states-and-egypt-advance-bilateral-trade-an.

[74] Barbara Kotschwar and Jeffrey J. Schott, *Reengaging Egypt: Options for US-Egypt Economic Relations*, Peterson Institute for International Economics, "In Brief", January 2010.

[75] For example, see Meredith Broadbent, "The Role of FTA Negotiations in the Future of U.S.-Egypt Relations," Center for Strategic and International Studies, December 2011, http://csis.org/files/publication/111212_Broadbent_USEgyptTrade_Web.pdf; Ahmed Galal and Robert Z. Lawrence, "Anchoring Reform with a U.S.-Egypt Free Trade Agreement," Policy Analyses in International Economics 74, Peterson Institute for International Economics, May 2005, http://bookstore.piie.com/book-store/3683.html.

Egyptian society, and not contribute to general improvement of Egypt's economic conditions and living standards.[76] Some industries, firms, and workers could be adversely affected if increased foreign competition results from an FTA or if particular provisions of the FTA disadvantage their interests.

Separately, the United States could focus on countries that currently are not undergoing political transitions. For example, the United States could renew FTA negotiations with the UAE. Additionally, the United States may consider negotiating regional investment and trade agreements, in order to bolster regional economic ties in addition to U.S.-MENA trade and investment.

Negotiating new FTAs may be complicated by the fact that Trade Promotion Authority (TPA) expired in 2007.[77] TPA is the authority Congress grants to the President to enter into certain FTAs and to have their implementing bills considered under expedited legislative procedures, provided they meet certain statutory obligations in negotiating them. The President could request and the 113th Congress could consider the renewal of TPA. Negotiating new BITs may have more momentum given the Obama Administration's conclusion of its review of the U.S. Model BIT in April 2012. The United States negotiates BITs on the basis of a model, which has been subject to periodic reviews and revisions. The Administration is resuming BIT negotiations previously halted during the Model BIT review.[78]

- **Updating existing FTAs and BITs:** Congress could consider updating the U.S. BITs with Egypt and Tunisia. Since these BITs came into effect, the U.S. Model BIT framework has been revised periodically, most recently in 2012. The Model BIT also serves as the template for investment provisions in current U.S. FTAs. Congress could also consider revising and "updating" the U.S.-Israel FTA. The U.S.-Israel FTA, signed and entered into force in 1985, was the first FTA ever entered into by the United States. Since then, the scope of issues discussed in trade negotiations has expanded. For example, the U.S.-Israel FTA does not contain provisions on electronic commerce and technical barriers to trade, has limited coverage of services and IPR, and has had limited effect on trade in agricultural products.[79]

- **Conducting oversight of existing FTAs:** Congress could examine existing U.S. FTAs in the region. In particular, it may be interested in examining how well they have achieved their objectives, and their impact on increasing and diversifying bilateral trade flows.

---

[76] Ibid.

[77] See CRS Report RL33743, *Trade Promotion Authority (TPA) and the Role of Congress in Trade Policy*, by J. F. Hornbeck and William H. Cooper.

[78] U.S. Department of State, "Model Bilateral Investment Treaty," press release, April 20, 2012, http://www.state.gov/r/pa/prs/ps/2012/04/188198.htm. See CRS Report RL33978, *The U.S. Bilateral Investment Treaty Program: An Overview*, by Martin A. Weiss and Shayerah Ilias Akhtar.

[79] Edward Gresser, *Update the Israel Free Trade Agreement*, The New Democratic Leadership Council, April 2010.

Multilateral Options

Congress additionally has multilateral tools at its disposal to foster economic ties with MENA countries. Trade policy at the multilateral level may yield benefits, such as requiring countries to adopt international rules, not available through unilateral or bilateral actions. Congress could encourage the United States to intensify existing efforts to support WTO accession for MENA countries such as Iraq, Libya, and Yemen, and provide technical assistance for countries working towards WTO accession. The United States could work with countries to fully implement their WTO accession commitments, such as through enhanced trade capacity building efforts. The United States could also cooperate more closely with the EU and other countries in international forums.

In May 2011, the G-8 launched the "Deauville Partnership with Arab Countries in Transition," a forum for coordinating assistance to "transitioning" MENA countries, currently defined by the Partnership to include Egypt, Jordan, Libya, Morocco, Tunisia, and Yemen. The Partnership also includes the G-8 countries, other countries from the region (Saudi Arabia, the United Arab Emirates, Qatar, Kuwait, Turkey), and several international financial institutions (IFIs). The Partnership is pursuing a number of policy tools to bolster sustainable, inclusive, growing economies in the region, and could be a fruitful avenue for coordinating with other countries on efforts to increase trade and investment with MENA countries. The current MENA-TIP initiative can be viewed as part of the U.S. contribution to international efforts under the trade and investment "track" of the Deauville Partnership.[80]

Issues for Congress: Possible Challenges and Implementation Questions

Congress may face a number of issues if it addresses policy options to facilitate greater U.S. trade and investment with the MENA region.

First, some analysts question whether increased trade and investment can support democratic political transitions. Current discussions for increasing trade and investment with the MENA region are rooted in the belief that these policy tools will bolster economic growth and help support the democratic political transitions occurring in the region. However, the link between trade and investment, on the one hand, and democracy, on the other, is contentious. Some experts argue that trade and investment promote governance; increase the size of the middle class; facilitate the flow of ideas; and develop institutions related to protection of property and rule of law, which in turn, it is argued, create popular pressure for democracy. [81] Additionally, some analysts argue that pursuing FTAs and BITs in particular with various MENA countries could help anchor reforms, such as related transparency, governance, and rule of law, that can provide foundations for democratic political transitions and institutions.[82]

---

[80] Meeting with USTR officials, January 10, 2013.

[81] For example, see Quan Li and Rafael Reuveny, "Economic Globalization and Democracy: An Empirical Analysis," Working Paper, 2000, http://www.international.ucla.edu/cms/files/GLODEM39.pdf.

[82] For example, see Ahmed Galal and Robert Z. Lawrence, "Anchoring Reform with a U.S.-Egypt Free Trade Agreement," Policy Analyses in International Economics 74, Peterson Institute for International Economics, May 2005, http://bookstore.piie.com/book-store/3683.html.

Others argue that the links between trade, investment, and democracy are not straightforward.[83] They argue that governments can gain legitimacy by opening their economies and securing economic growth, without reforming or opening politically. They cite a number of economies that have opened to the world economically while sustaining governments that are not fully democratic; China is often cited as an example in this context. This raises questions about whether trade and investment could be effective in helping Arab countries transition to more democratic political systems. Additionally, some analysts question whether protestors in various MENA countries want greater trade and investment ties. In Egypt, for example, public opinion indicates that many believe that the economic liberalization pursued under the old regime enabled corruption and exacerbated economic inequality.[84]

Second, questions abound about whether U.S. trade policy tools could be effective in overcoming the obstacles to greater U.S. trade and investment in the MENA region. Some analysts question whether trade and/or investment liberalizing agreements will result in increased U.S. trade and investment to the MENA region. According to the U.S. Commercial Service, some of the greatest obstacles to U.S. firms hoping to do business in MENA countries relate to corruption, transparency, governance, rule of law, and bureaucratic red tape, among others. Some argue that completing FTAs or BITs, or encouraging countries to join the WTO, could help MENA governments push through reforms that address many of these impediments. Others express concern that even if such reforms are pursued in the context of FTA, BIT, or WTO negotiations, there could be implementation problems, and that U.S. trade and investment with MENA countries and the region could remain limited. Additionally, a number of factors affect investment and trade flows beyond government policies, including the market size, economic growth, labor force, endowment of natural resources, political stability, and infrastructure, among others, which raise questions about how effective policy options could be at dramatically increasing trade and investment flows.

In addition, the capacity of federal export finance and other promotion agencies to support U.S. trade and investment in the MENA may be limited. For instance, while Ex-Im Bank and OPIC could work to incentivize exports to the MENA region, U.S. firms' interest in doing business the MENA region will drive their demand for Ex-Im Bank and OPIC financing.

Third, if an agenda of increased trade and investment is further pursued, a host of questions arise that may be considered in implementing this policy agenda. For example:

- **Timing:** The political situation in some MENA countries is highly uncertain. Should the United States wait to enhance its trade and investment ties in the region until the political situation stabilizes? Or should the United States continue to enhance trade and investment ties sooner, in order to facilitate political outcomes it views as favorable? If the United States delays engagement, will others—such as EU countries, Turkey, and China—take advantage of business opportunities in the region sooner, depressing opportunities for U.S. businesses?

---

[83] For example, see Catharin E. Dalpino, "Does Globalization Promote Democracy?: An Early Assessment," Brookings, Fall 2001, http://www.brookings.edu/articles/2001/fall_democracy_dalpino.aspx.

[84] James V. Grimaldi and Robert O'Harrow Jr., "In Egypt, corruption cases had an American root," *Washington Post*, October 19, 2011; and, Economist Intelligence Unit, "Country Report: Egypt," November 2011.

- **Region-Wide Policies vs. Country-Specific Policies:** Current U.S. trade and investment policy is quite diverse across countries in the MENA region, and the MENA economies themselves are quite heterogeneous. Should the United States pursue a region-wide agenda of increasing trade and investment, while tailoring policies to fit the individual needs of specific countries? For example, some argue that Egypt and Tunisia are better positioned than, say, Libya, to enter FTA negotiations with the United States, because they are members of the WTO and have BITs with the United States, while Libya only has WTO observer status and is experiencing political upheaval. While WTO accession is not explicitly required for the United States to negotiate BITs or FTAs with a country, U.S. trade agreements generally build on WTO commitments, and WTO membership is viewed as a stepping stone to a FTA.

- **Cooperation with the EU:** In his May 2011 speech on MENA, President Obama suggested that U.S. efforts to increase trade and investment in the region would be pursued cooperatively with the EU. Such cooperation efforts are underway, and questions arise about the scope, and depth of the cooperation. In the past, the United States and the EU have adopted different approaches in the MENA. For example, under the MEFTA effort during the Bush Administration, the United States negotiated comprehensive FTAs with individual countries with the goal that such efforts would expand into a region-wide free trade area agreement. In contrast, the EU adopted a more regional approach to economic integration from the start. Other factors may complicate cooperation. For example, the United States and the EU have differing views on regulatory policy and standards, and some view U.S. and EU businesses as competitors in the MENA region. Finally, some of these countries already have strong economic ties with the EU and want to develop closer economies ties with the United States, as was the case with the U.S.-Morocco FTA.

  U.S.-EU cooperation on the MENA region could expand should the United States and the EU launch negotiations on a Transatlantic Trade and Investment Partnership. As an example of the potential for future collaboration, the "Joint Principles for International Investment" and the "Joint Principles for Information and Communication Technology (ICT) Services"—agreed to bilaterally by the United States with Morocco and Jordan—were modeled after U.S.-EU agreements.[85]

- **Congressional Interest:** In October 2011, Congress approved the implementing legislation for FTAs with Colombia, South Korea, and Panama, years after the agreements were formally negotiated.[86] Will their approval provide momentum for further FTA negotiations, or does their lengthy approval point to the polarization in Congress regarding future FTAs? How should Congress prioritize FTAs in the MENA region with ongoing trade negotiations, including with regards to the Trans-Pacific Partnership (TPP) and a potential Transatlantic Trade

---

[85] Discussion with USTR official, January 10, 2013.

[86] For more on these FTAs, see CRS Report RL34470, *The U.S.-Colombia Free Trade Agreement: Background and Issues*, by M. Angeles Villarreal; CRS Report R41534, *The EU-South Korea Free Trade Agreement and Its Implications for the United States*, by William H. Cooper et al.; and CRS Report RL32540, *The U.S.-Panama Free Trade Agreement*, by J. F. Hornbeck.

and Investment Partnership?[87] How should Congress prioritize countries within the MENA region for FTAs? Trade promotion authority (TPA) likely will play a major role in any future FTA negotiation with MENA countries.

Outlook

U.S. trade policy responses to political change in the MENA can be characterized as incremental and long-term—focused on creating "building blocks" that could potentially lead to larger-scale trade and investment agreements in the future. For example, present USTR engagement with Egypt is centered on making the country's business environment more conducive to trade and investment. Such efforts could pave the way for FTA negotiations in the future, though this is not necessarily a current goal for the Administration.[88]

Going forward, any trade policy agenda pursued by U.S. policymakers in the region could be affected by a host of external factors, including the following:

- U.S. trade and investment relationships in the region are diverse, resulting in different "starting points" for engagement.[89] At one end of the spectrum, Libya is not yet a member of the WTO, which many view as a starting point for further U.S. engagement. At the other end of the spectrum, the United States has well-established trade relationships with Morocco and Jordan—which include a bilateral FTA with each country—that serve as a foundation for the recent bilateral agreements on principles on investment and ICT services under the MENA-TIP.

- Countries in the region have markedly diverse economic situations and priorities. Some countries, such as Egypt, are more focused on maintaining macroeconomic stability over the short-term, delaying longer-term initiatives, including trade and investment liberalization. Other countries with more stable economic conditions may be able to engage more effectively with the United States on trade policy issues.[90]

- Ongoing political uncertainty in some countries can make it challenging to negotiate on trade policy—or even, more fundamentally, know with whom to negotiate. For instance, despite the longstanding U.S.-Egyptian bilateral relationship, it is difficult for U.S. trade negotiators to know with whom to negotiate on the Egyptian side, giving the fluid nature of Egypt's political situation. As another example, political uncertainty also can make it more difficult for Foreign Commercial Service staff to operate in the region.[91] In contrast, Tunisia's relatively "smoother" transition has facilitated U.S. engagement with Tunisia under the re-invigorated TIFA process.[92]

---

[87] For more on TPP, CRS Report R42694, *The Trans-Pacific Partnership Negotiations and Issues for Congress*, coordinated by Ian F. Fergusson.

[88] Meeting with USTR officials, January 10, 2013.

[89] Ibid.

[90] Ibid.

[91] ITA response to CRS inquiry, February 8, 2013.

[92] Meeting with USTR officials, January 10, 2013.

- U.S. trade policy responses are affected by the demand of U.S. companies for doing business in certain areas of the world. While agencies such as OPIC, Ex-Im Bank, and TDA can choose to make supporting U.S. commercial activity in the region a top priority and make resources available for this purpose, U.S. businesses will take advantage of the financing and funding only if they have sufficient commercial incentives to do so.

Depending on the type of trade policy responses pursued in the region, questions may arise about the effectiveness of policy tools used to promote increased trade and investment, as well as their impact on political transitions, and how quickly their benefits would be borne out. Additionally, how these policies are designed could have substantial implications for U.S. interests. However, in a constrained budgetary environment, trade and investment may be attractive policy tools compared to other options, such as foreign aid, for supporting economic development in MENA countries—as well as encouraging transparency, governance, and other reforms in the region—while also potentially creating new economic opportunities for U.S. businesses.

Appendix. Trade Tables

Figure A-1. U.S. Exports to MENA Countries/Territories, 2011

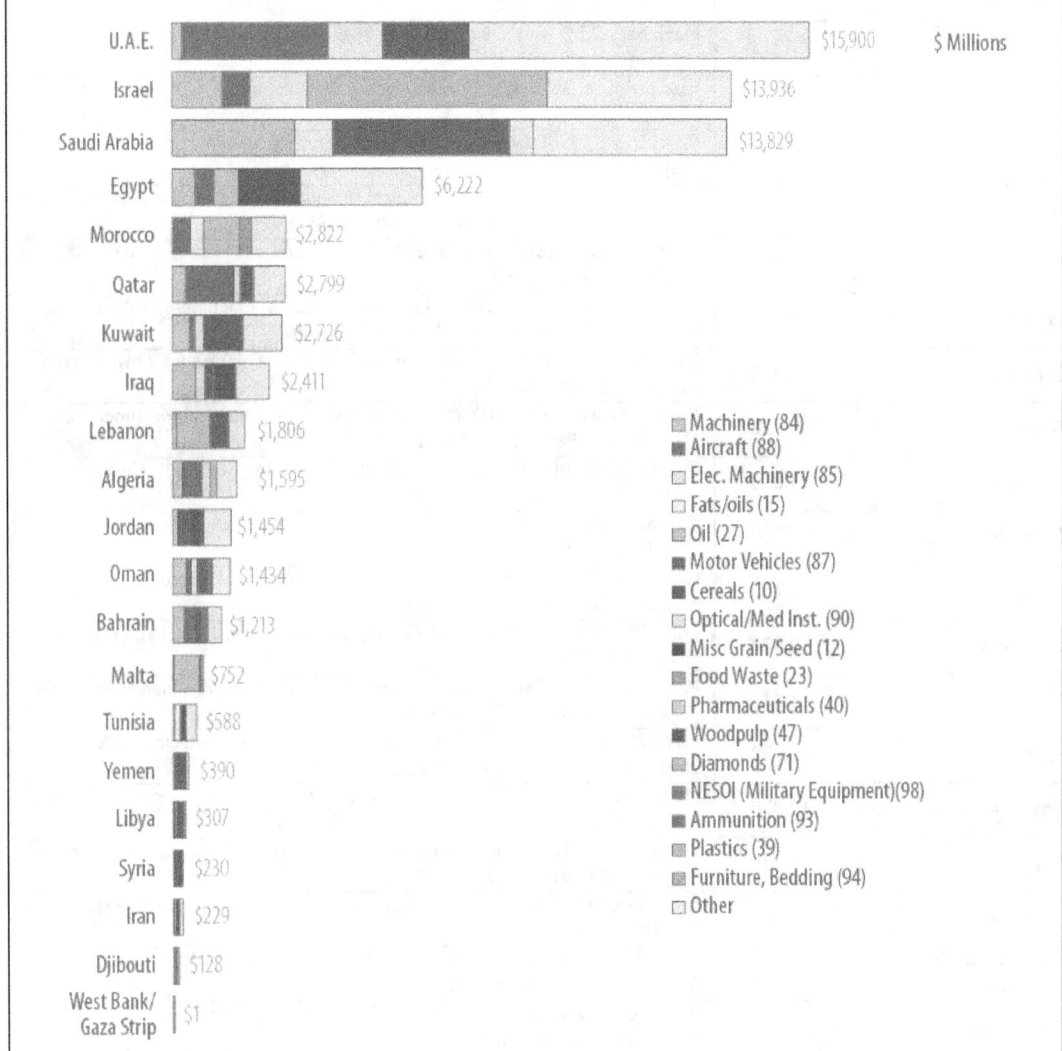

Source: Global Trade Atlas.

Notes: Harmonized Tariff Schedule (HTS) numbers in parentheses in legend. NEOSI = Not elsewhere specified or included.

Table A-1. Top U.S. Exports to MENA Countries/Territories, 2011

Country	Total Exports ($ Millions)	Major U.S. Exports and Shares of Total (with Harmonized Tariff Schedule [HTS] Numbers)
Algeria	1,595	Aircraft Parts, 30% (88) Machinery, 15% (84); Electrical Machinery, 13% (85); and Oil, 10% (27)=68%
Bahrain	1,213	Machinery 23%, (84); Aircraft Parts, 20% (88); NESOI, 15% (98); Motor Vehicles 13% (87)=71%
Djibouti	128	Fats and Oils, 28% (15); Cereals, 24% (10); Machinery, 12% (84); Electrical Machinery, 7% (85) =71%
Egypt	6,222	Cereals, 24% (10); Oil, 10% (27); Machinery, 9% (84); Aircraft Parts, 8% (88)=51%
Iran	229	Woodpulp, 25% (47); Pharmaceutical Products, 17% (30); Plastics, 13% (39); Optical, Medical Instruments, 10% (90)=65%
Iraq	2,411	Machinery, 24% (84); Cereals, 23%, (10); Electrical Machinery, 10% (85); Motor Vehicles, 9% (87)=66%
Israel	13,936	Precious Stones (Diamonds), 43% (71); Electrical Machinery, 10% (85); Machinery, 9% (84); Aircraft Parts, 5% (88)=67%
Jordan	1,454	Motor Vehicles, 21% (87); Cereals, 18% (10); Machinery, 9% (84); Arms and Ammunition, 6% (93)=54%
Kuwait	2,726	Motor Vehicles, 36% (87); Machinery, 16% (84); Electrical Machinery, 8% (85); Aircraft Parts, 5% (88)=65%
Lebanon	1,806	Oil, 46% (27); Motor Vehicles, 23% (87); Machinery, 6% (84); Cereals, 4% (10)=79%
Libya	307	Cereals, 56% (10); Motor Vehicles, 16% (87); Machinery, 8% (84); Fats and Oils, 5% (15)=85%
Malta	752	Oil, 86% (27); Aircraft Parts, 3% (88); Optical/Medical Instruments, 3% (90); NESOI (Military Equipment) 2% (98)=94%
Morocco	2,822	Oil, 32% (27); Aircraft Parts, 16% (88); Fats and Oils, 12% (15); Food Waste, 10%, (23)=70%
Oman	1,434	Machinery, 23% (84); Motor Vehicles, 22% (87); Electrical Machinery, 10% (85); Aircraft Parts, 9% (88)=64%
Qatar	2,799	Aircraft Parts, 43% (88); Machinery, 12% (84); Motor Vehicles, 12% (87); Electrical Machinery, 6% (85)=73%
Saudi Arabia	13,829	Motor Vehicles, 32% (87); Machinery, 22% (84); Electrical Machinery, 7% (85); Medical, Surgical Instruments, 4% (90); =65%
Syria	230	Cereals, 64% (10); Grain, Seeds, 26% (12); Optical/Medical Instruments, 3% (90) Food Waste, 3% (23); =97%
Tunisia	588	Fats and Oils, 22% (15); Grain, Seeds, 21% (12); Machinery, 8% (84); Cereals, 5% (10) =56%
United Arab Emirates	15,900	Aircraft Parts, 23% (88); Machinery, 16% (84); Motor Vehicles, 14% (87); Electrical Machinery, 8% (85)=61%
West Bank	1	Machinery, 62% (84); Furniture and Bedding, 14% (94); Seeds, Grain, 8% (12); Motor Vehicles, 7% (87)=91%
Gaza Strip	.05	Machinery, 89% (84);Electrical Machinery, 6% (85); Aircraft Parts, 5% (88)=100%
Yemen	390	Cereals, 47%, (10); Motor Vehicles, 23% (87); Machinery, 8% (84); Pharmaceuticals 4% (30)=82%
TOTAL	70,772	

Source: Global Trade Atlas.

Note: NEOSI = Not elsewhere specified or included.

Figure A-2. U.S. Imports from MENA Countries/Territories, 2011

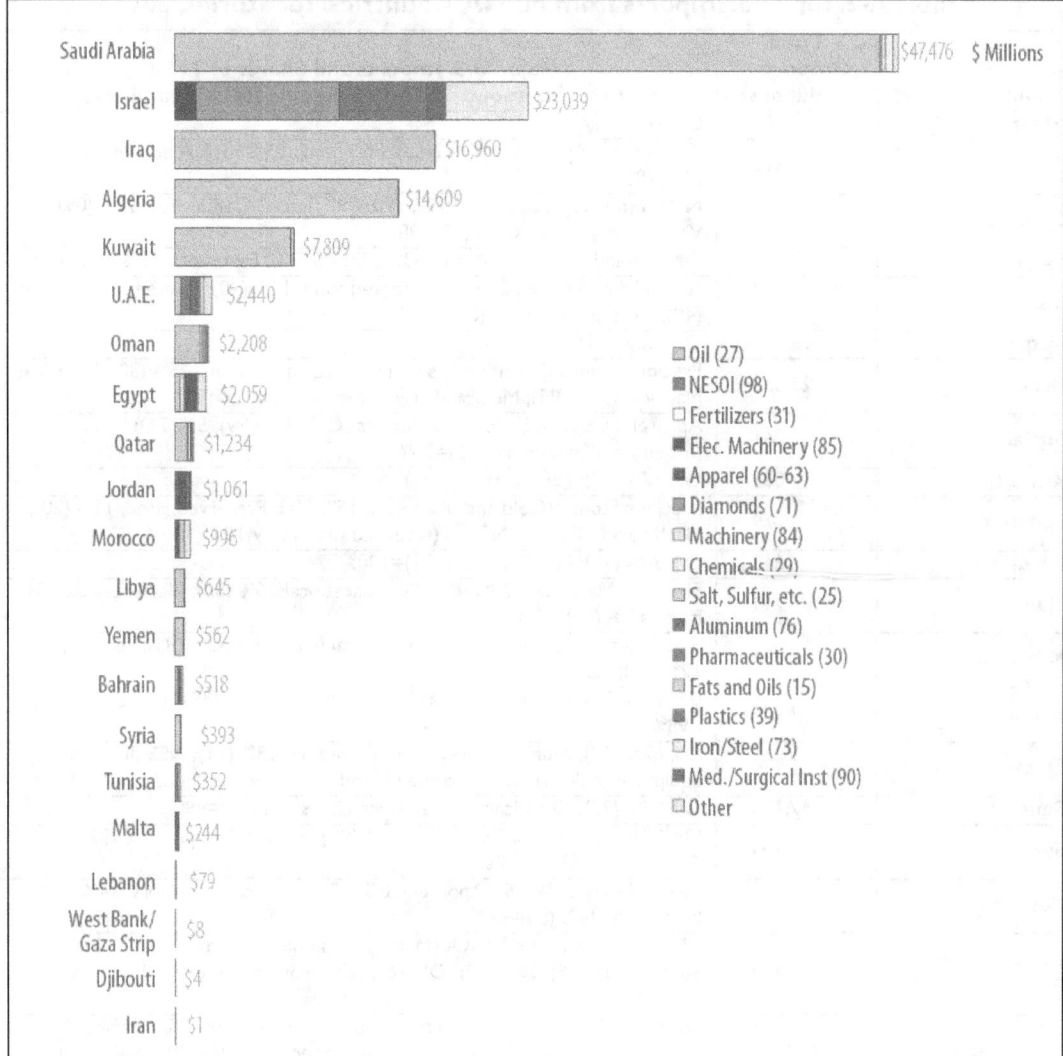

Source: Global Trade Atlas.

Notes: Harmonized Tariff Schedule (HTS) numbers in parentheses in legend. NEOSI = Not elsewhere specified or included.

Table A-2. Top U.S. Imports from MENA Countries/Territories, 2011

Country	Total Imports ($ Millions)	Major U.S. Imports and Shares of Total (with Harmonized Tariff Schedule [HTS] Numbers)
Algeria	14,609	Oil, 100% (27)
Bahrain	518	Textiles and Apparel, 34% (61-63), Fertilizers, 29% (31); Aluminum, 19% (76))=82%
Djibouti	4	NESOI (military equipment) 77% (98 -99); Spices, Coffee, Tea, 20% (09); Vegetables and roots, 1% (07)=98
Egypt	2,059	Textiles and Apparel, 43% (61-63); oil, 17% (27); Fertilizers, 13% (31)=73%
Iran	1	Art and Antiques, 80%, (97); Preserved food, 11% (20); Printed Materials, 6% (49); Nuts and Fruit 2% (08)=99%
Iraq	16,960	Oil 100% (27)
Israel	23,039	Precious Stones (Diamonds), 41% (71); Pharmaceuticals, 25% (30); Electrical Machinery, 6% (85); Medical, Surgical Instruments, 5% (90)=77%
Jordan	1,061	Apparel, 85% (62-63); Precious Stones (Gold Jewelry), 5% (71); NESOI (military equipment, 4% (98)=94%
Kuwait	7,809	Oil, 97% (27); Fertilizers, 2% (31);=99%
Lebanon	79	Precious Stones (Gold and diamonds),15% (71); Preserved Food, 15% (20); Machinery, 14% (84); NESOI (returned machinery)10% (98)=54%
Libya	645	Oil, 96% (27); Fertilizers, 4% (31)=100%
Malta	244	Electrical Machinery, 73% (85); Pharmaceuticals, 9% (30); Machinery 5% (84); Fabrics 2% (60)= 89%
Morocco	996	Salt, Sulfur (Calcium), 30% (25); Electrical Machinery,13% (85); Fertilizers, 12% (31); Apparel, 7% (62)=62%
Oman	2,208	Oil, 76% (27); Precious Stones, 8% (71);); Plastic, 7% (39);Fertilizers, 7% (31) =98%
Qatar	1,234	Oil, 67% (27); Aluminum, 14% (76); Fertilizers, 13% (31); NESOI (military equipment being returned to the United States for repair), 2% (98)=96%
Saudi Arabia	47,476	Oil, 97% (27); Chemicals, 1% (29); Fertilizers, 1% (31)=99%
Syria	393	Oil, 93% (27); Spices, Coffee, Tea, 3% (09) Art and Antiques, 1% (97); Apparel, 1% (61) =100%
Tunisia	352	Fats and Oils, 21% (15); Apparel, 20% (62); Electrical Machinery, 14% (85); Machinery, 11% (84)=66%
United Arab Emirates	2,439	Aluminum, 27% (76); NESOI (Military equipment returned to the United States for repair), 26% (98); Oil, 16% (27); Iron and Steel Products, 8% (73);=77%
West Bank	5	NESOI (Military Equipment returned to the United States for repair), 38% (99); Fats and Oils, 28% (15); Grains and Seeds, 18% (12); Vegetables and roots 6% (07)=84%
Gaza Strip	3	Woven Apparel, 99% (61)
Yemen	562	Oil, 100% (27)
TOTAL	$122,696	

Source: Global Trade Atlas.

Notes: NEOSI = Not elsewhere specified or included.

Author Contact Information

Rebecca M. Nelson, Coordinator
Analyst in International Trade and Finance
rnelson@crs.loc.gov, 7-6819

Mary Jane Bolle
Specialist in International Trade and Finance
mjbolle@crs.loc.gov, 7-7753

Shayerah Ilias Akhtar
Specialist in International Trade and Finance
silias@crs.loc.gov, 7-9253